The Founding of the State of Israel

The Founding of the State of Israel

Other books in the At Issue in History series:

The Founding of the State of Israel

Mitchell Bard, *Book Editor*

Daniel Leone, *President*
Bonnie Szumski, *Publisher*
Scott Barbour, *Managing Editor*

OPPOSING
VIEWPOINTS® AT ISSUE IN HISTORY
SERIES

GREENHAVEN
PRESS®

THOMSON
—————※—————™
GALE

San Diego • Detroit • New York • San Francisco • Cleveland
New Haven, Conn. • Waterville, Maine • London • Munich

THOMSON

━━━━━✦━━━━━™

GALE

LIBRARY OF CONGRESS CATALOGING-IN-PUBLICATION DATA

The founding of the state of Israel / Mitchell Bard, book editor.
    p. cm. — (At issue in history)
Includes bibliographical references and index.
ISBN 0-7377-1349-6 (pbk. : alk. paper) — ISBN 0-7377-1348-8 (lib. : alk. paper)
    1. Palestine—History—1917–1948. 2. Palestine—Politics and government—1917–1948. 3. Zionism—Government policy—Great Britain—History. 4. Jewish-Arab relations—History—1917–1948. I. Series.
DS126.F68 2003
956.94'04—dc21
                                               2002034683

Printed in the United States of America

Contents

Chapter 2: Partition and War: The Birth of Israel

Chapter 3: Looking Back at the Creation of Israel

Foreword

Historian Robert Weiss defines history simply as "a record and interpretation of past events." Both elements—record and interpretation—are necessary, Weiss argues.

> Names, dates, places, and events are the essence of history. But historical writing is not a compendium of facts. It consists of facts placed in a sequence to tell a connected story. A work of history is not merely a story, however. It also must analyze what happened and *why*—that is, it must interpret the past for the reader.

For example, the events of December 7, 1941, that led President Franklin D. Roosevelt to call it "a date which will live in infamy" are fairly well known and straightforward. A force of Japanese planes and submarines launched a torpedo and bombing attack on American military targets in Pearl Harbor, Hawaii. The surprise assault sank five battleships, disabled or sank fourteen additional ships, and left almost twenty-four hundred American soldiers and sailors dead. On the following day, the United States formally entered World War II when Congress declared war on Japan.

These facts and consequences were almost immediately communicated to the American people who heard reports about Pearl Harbor and President Roosevelt's response on the radio. All realized that this was an important and pivotal event in American and world history. Yet the news from Pearl Harbor raised many unanswered questions. Why did Japan decide to launch such an offensive? Why were the attackers so successful in catching America by surprise? What did the attack reveal about the two nations, their people, and their leadership? What were its causes, and what were its effects? Political leaders, academic historians, and students look to learn the basic facts of historical events and to read the intepretations of these events by many different sources, both primary and secondary, in order to develop a more complete picture of the event in a historical context.

In the case of Pearl Harbor, several important questions surrounding the event remain in dispute, most notably the role of President Roosevelt. Some historians have blamed his policies for deliberately provoking Japan to attack in order to propel America into World War II; a few have gone so far as to accuse him of knowing of the impending attack but not informing others. Other historians, examining the same event, have exonerated the president of such charges, arguing that the historical evidence does not support such a theory.

The Greenhaven At Issue in History series recognizes that many important historical events have been interpreted differently and in some cases remain shrouded in controversy. Each volume features a collection of articles that focus on a topic that has sparked controversy among eyewitnesses, contemporary observers, and historians. An introductory essay sets the stage for each topic by presenting background and context. Several chapters then examine different facets of the subject at hand with readings chosen for their diversity of opinion. Each selection is preceded by a summary of the author's main points and conclusions. A bibliography is included for those students interested in pursuing further research. An annotated table of contents and thorough index help readers to quickly locate material of interest. Taken together, the contents of each of the volumes in the Greenhaven At Issue in History series will help students become more discriminating and thoughtful readers of history.

Introduction

For the Jewish people the founding of Israel represented nothing less than a miracle, the rebirth of their independent homeland, from which they were driven two thousand years earlier. It was all the more significant due to its timing, coming just a few years after the Holocaust, the most cataclysmic event in Jewish history. For Arabs, Israel's founding was something else entirely. Rather than a miracle it was (and continues to be) viewed as a disaster that led to the dispersion of hundreds of thousands of Palestinian Arabs and the insinuation of an unwanted Jewish outpost in the Arab and Muslim heartland.

The modern history of Israel is one defined primarily by conflict as the Jews fought the imperial rulers of their homeland—the British—the native inhabitants of the area, and the surrounding Arab nations for the right to reestablish their nation. The Arabs did everything in their power to prevent the Jews from achieving their national aspirations and, to this day, most have not given up the struggle to reverse what happened in 1948 when Israel's statehood was formally declared.

A Long History

It may appear that the Jews suddenly showed up in the Middle East in the twentieth century and demanded to have a state of their own, but this is not accurate. The Jewish people have maintained a connection to their ancestral homeland for more than thirty-seven hundred years. In fact Jews trace their claim to the land of Israel to the biblical promise made by God to Abraham to make his descendants a great nation in the land between the Nile and Euphrates (Genesis 12: 1–2). For people with deep religious convictions, this biblical connection is enough. For those more concerned with history and politics, though, this is not a convincing argument for the Jewish people's right to the land. But the biblical promise is not the only basis for the Jewish people's claim. They can also point to the fact that they created the first independent nation in the region of the Promised Land around 1000 B.C. when the twelve Jewish tribes that emerged from slavery in Egypt united to form the world's first constitutional monarchy.

Throughout the following centuries, the Jews continued to maintain a presence in the region, although they were conquered and exiled by various powers, including the Assyrians, the Babylonians, the Greeks, and the Romans. After Muhammad died in 632 his followers marched out of Arabia and proceeded to create a great empire stretching across the Middle East (including Palestine) and North Africa and into Spain. It is at this point, at the earliest, that Arabs can make any claim to the land of Israel. For thirteen hundred years the Muslims ruled the region, but they never established any political entity in Palestine. In fact for most of Muslim history the area was considered a backwater and was largely neglected.

The Rise of Zionism

Throughout the centuries, Jewish communities grew and contracted depending on the degree of tolerance of the rulers. Under Muslim rule, large numbers of Jews were not allowed to return to the land, and the rulers made sure that those who did live under their governments remained powerless. When the Ottoman Turks conquered the area in the sixteenth century, they treated the Jews with relative tolerance and the community slowly began to grow. In the nineteenth century more Jews, particularly those who were orthodox, began to establish communities in Israel.

At the same time the situation in much of the Christian world was bad for the Jews—and growing worse. Throughout centuries of Christian expansion Jews had experienced varying degrees of anti-Semitism. By the mid-nineteenth century several Jewish thinkers began to conclude that there was no way to eradicate this hatred and that the only way to insure Jewish safety and survival was to establish a homeland where the Jews would control their own destiny. The belief that the Jews were a nation like any other, and that they had a right to self-determination in their homeland, became known as Zionism.

Zionism came in a variety of "flavors." For example, practical Zionists focused their efforts on settling the land. Religious Zionists believed the Jewish homeland should be based on Jewish law. Socialist Zionists were interested in establishing a just society. Messianic Zionists thought that establishing a Jewish state would help to usher in the messianic age. A small minority of Jews, though, based on their view that the Messiah had to come first before the Jews could return to their homeland, adopted an anti-Zionist position.

Many of these positions were theoretical or philosophical. But a Viennese journalist named Theodor Herzl set out to implement the creation of a Jewish state and founded what may be called political Zionism. For Herzl the key to independence was to win international backing and legal recognition for a Jewish state. Herzl founded the World Zionist Organization, which held its first conference in Basel, Switzerland, in 1897, and announced the goal of the Zionist movement was the creation of a Jewish state in Palestine.

Some people believed the situation for Jews was so perilous that it was important to establish a haven to protect them immediately, no matter where. Herzl initially joined in this view and negotiated with the British who, at one point, intimated they might be prepared to allow the Jews to establish their state in Uganda. The idea of settling anywhere other than the land of Israel caused a rift in the Zionist movement in 1903.

The Uganda plan never got very far. Herzl was persuaded that he had made a mistake and, after having considered this alternative as a temporary solution, joined the overwhelming majority in the organization that insisted the only place for a Jewish state was in the Promised Land.

Waves of Immigrants

Jews had longed to return to their homeland throughout the centuries, and the timing for finally doing so became ripe in the late nineteenth and early twentieth centuries. The new political Zionist movement encouraged many to return home, and the persecution of Jewish communities in various parts of the world forced others to seek a safe haven. In addition the Muslim empire was slowly crumbling, and the Turkish rulers were gradually losing their ability to prevent the building of a Jewish community in Israel.

While Herzl was politicking, attacks on Jews in Russia helped provoke large-scale immigration to Palestine. This was one of a series of waves of immigration. The first wave

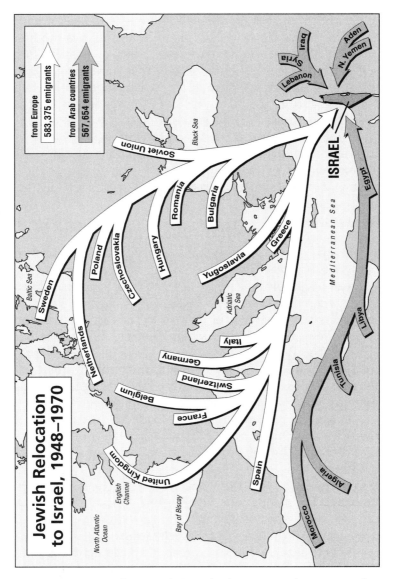

Jewish Relocation to Israel, 1948–1970

from Europe
583,375 emigrants

from Arab countries
567,654 emigrants

of about twenty thousand Jews had come in the 1880s, also provoked by anti-Semitism abroad. This is referred to as the First Aliyah. The word *aliyah* literally means "to go up" and is applied to Jews who move to Israel because they are viewed as moving closer to God.

After a new series of pogroms in Russia at the beginning of the twentieth century, a second wave of forty thousand immigrants arrived between 1904 and 1914. These were many of the socialist Zionists who founded the first agricultural collectives known as kibbutzim (Degania was the first in 1909). These settlers started newspapers, created the first self-defense organization to protect themselves from Arab marauders, and revived the Hebrew language (which had been restricted to use in prayers and now was adopted as the everyday method of communication).

The native Arabs viewed the growing presence of Jews in what they considered their homeland with growing alarm. Sometimes their opposition was voiced in political forums, but other times it was expressed in violence against the Jewish pioneers.

The Balfour Declaration

By the end of the Second Aliyah World War I had broken out. By this time Herzl had died and been replaced as the political leader of the Zionist movement by a Russian-born Englishman named Chaim Weizmann. A chemist by training, Weizmann lobbied the British to support the creation of an independent Jewish state in Palestine. On November 2, 1917, the British notified the Zionists, in a letter from foreign secretary Arthur James Balfour to Lord Rothschild, that the proposals they had submitted were acceptable. This came to be known as the Balfour Declaration.

The main reason the British made the declaration at that time was that they needed to bring the United States into the war. They believed American Jews had a great deal of influence on U.S. foreign policy and that they would use it to pressure the American government to enter the war in exchange for the Balfour Declaration. The United States did join the fight with Britain, but for its own reasons and not because of the Jews or the declaration.

As part of the war effort the British were determined to defeat the Turks and dismantle the Ottoman Empire. To do this they believed they needed the help of the Arabs in Arabia. They secretly negotiated with one of the key leaders of the Arabs, Hussein ibn Ali. The British promised to give Arabs independence in conquered Turkish territories if ibn Ali led his people in a revolt against the Ottoman Empire. He agreed, and his forces helped the British win the war in the Middle East.

Great Britain and France (which had also fought the Turks) emerged as the major powers in the Middle East after the collapse of the Ottoman Empire. While they had promised the Arabs independence in most of the Middle East, the British and French had left Palestine out of the areas pledged to become sovereign Arab territory. They also had decided that nations must be able to sustain themselves before becoming autonomous, and they determined that the Arabs were not yet ready. To help nations prepare for independence the great powers devised the mandate system. Though in truth, Britain and France hoped to maintain control over the Middle East for their own purposes.

The British Mandate

When the San Remo Conference that followed the end of World War I convened on April 24, 1920, France and Great Britain implemented a secret agreement they had made during the war to divvy up the Ottoman Empire. France was given the mandate for Syria, and Great Britain was given the mandate for Iraq and Palestine. The mandate for Palestine, which included the Balfour Declaration, was formalized by the League of Nations on September 23, 1922.

The British recognized that the mandates contradicted their agreements with the Arabs; consequently, they made every effort to placate the Arab leaders by installing them as puppet rulers over territories under their control. Britain created an entirely new province by severing almost 80 percent of historic Palestine east of the Jordan River and calling it Transjordan (now called Jordan).

Many Jews were furious about the mandate, especially after Transjordan was lopped off from what they believed to be their homeland. Still, most Zionists were happy because the mandate included the Balfour Declaration, and the international community's recognition of the mandate was viewed as giving their goal even greater political legitimacy.

At the end of World War I the Jewish population was still only about 90,000, compared with 600,000 Arabs. After the war the Third Aliyah, stimulated largely by the Russian Revolution, brought another 40,000 Jews to Palestine. This group helped develop the country, draining malarial swamps and building towns. During this period the underground military defense force known as the Haganah was created, as was the first Jewish labor union movement, the Histadrut.

With official sanction of the mandate the Jews began to place a higher priority on developing the structure for a state—including a political body to make decisions for the community, expansion of rural and urban development, and most important, the expansion of the population. In the 1920s, the goal of increasing the Jewish population was again aided by a combination of anti-Semitism and economic hardship, this time primarily in Poland. The Fourth Aliyah was the result, bringing in about 80,000 more Jews, mostly from the middle class, who subsequently helped build the economy of Palestine.

A final large wave of 250,000 immigrants arrived in the decade from 1929 to 1939. This group, which included many professionals who helped build towns and industry, came as a result of the persecution of Jews by German chancellor Adolf Hitler.

Arabs Revolt

The Arab population of Palestine was extremely unhappy about the waves of Jewish immigrants, whom they saw as foreigners invading their country and stealing their land. They complained bitterly—first to the Turks and then to the British mandatory authorities. The Zionists made some efforts to negotiate with the Arabs and to find a way to coexist, but they were not successful. The Arabs turned to violence, instigated largely by the religious leader known as the Mufti of Jerusalem, Haj Amin el-Hussaini.

Beginning in 1921 the Mufti provoked the first of several riots against the Jews in an effort to force the British to terminate the Balfour Declaration and restrict Jewish immigration. A second major riot, in 1929, led to the massacre of Jews from the ancient town of Hebron, the place where Jewish patriarchs were believed to be buried. Jews who survived were forced to leave the city and would not return for more than four decades (Jews reestablished a presence in the city several years after Hebron was captured by Israeli forces in the Six-Day War of 1967). In 1936 a more sustained revolt, lasting three years, was mounted by the Arabs.

Each time the Arabs rioted the British launched an investigation. Commissions went to Palestine and heard Arab complaints that the Jews were stealing their land and driving them out of Palestine. In fact, all the land the Jews owned was purchased, usually at exorbitant prices, from wealthy landowners who lived outside Palestine. Moreover, the commissions usually found that the Arabs benefited from the Jewish settlement because it improved the standard of living in the country by enhancing the economy and providing better health care. Consequently, it actually stimulated Arab immigration into Palestine. Though the commissions essentially found the Arab claims groundless, they still recommended, in a series of "white papers," that Jewish immigration be curtailed in the hope of pacifying the Arabs. This tactic did not work.

Dividing Palestine

In 1937 a British commission led by former secretary of state Lord Earl Peel was sent to Palestine to investigate. The commission came to the conclusion that the best solution to the problem was to divide the country into two states, an Arab state and a Jewish state. It seemed logical that if two people were fighting over one land, it should be divided between them. The Arabs rejected the plan, known as the Peel Plan. They would never share "their" land with the Jews. The idea divided the Jews. Many were willing to accept the compromise solution, but others believed they were entitled to a state in all of Palestine. The British shelved the plan.

In the meantime one Zionist, Vladimir Jabotinsky, viewed Peel's partition idea as another step away from the Balfour Declaration. He insisted that the Jews should still get a state in all of historic Palestine—including the part that had been sliced away to create Transjordan. He argued that the British would never fulfill their promise to create a homeland and that the Jews would have to fight to achieve their aspirations. Toward that end, some of his followers split off from the Haganah, which had functioned purely as a self-defense force. They created a more militant organization known as the Irgun, which began to take offensive actions against the Arabs and later the British.

With the failure of the Peel Plan, the British resorted to their usual policy of restricting Jewish immigration, but this did nothing to assuage the anger felt by the Arabs, and their revolt continued into 1939. That year Jewish immigration more than doubled as Jews sought to flee Nazi Germany and what would become a world war began with the German invasion of Poland.

The British then issued a white paper announcing that the new government policy was to establish an Arab state in Palestine within ten years. Furthermore, Jewish immigration would be limited to no more than seventy-five thousand immigrants over the following five years, and none would be allowed after that without Arab permission. The declaration was a complete abandonment of the Balfour promise. Worse yet it severely restricted immigration in the short run and put the long-term decision in the hands of the Arabs at the very moment when the need for Jews to escape from Europe was growing more urgent.

The Jews Declare War

The Jews were torn. As the war in Europe expanded to a world war and the fate of the Jews became more precarious, the Jews in Palestine were determined to fight Hitler. At the same time, they could not tolerate the repudiation of the Balfour Declaration. The leader of the Jewish community, David Ben-Gurion, announced, "We must assist the British in the war as if there were no White Paper and we must resist the White Paper as if there were no war."

Many Jews joined the fight against the Nazis. They also reaffirmed their commitment to the establishment of a Jewish state at a meeting of Zionists at the Biltmore Hotel in New York in 1942. At the same time the Jews in Palestine did everything they could to illegally smuggle immigrants into the country. As the news of the Holocaust began to seep out, this effort became imperative. The British were equally determined, however, to prevent more Jews than were allowed according to their quota from entering Palestine, thereby dooming thousands, perhaps millions, to death at the hands of the Nazis.

Jews in Palestine fighting the British also became more militant. Another splinter group known as the Stern Gang (after its founder Avraham Stern) began to terrorize the British and assassinated one of their government officials in Cairo in 1944. The violent attacks by the Irgun and the Stern Gang were condemned by Jewish leaders in Palestine, who still used the Haganah primarily as a defensive force to protect Jewish communities from attacks by Arabs. The violence nevertheless escalated, with the most dramatic attack being the bombing of the King David Hotel by the Irgun in 1946. A part of the hotel was used as a headquarters for the British military, and the Irgun had issued warnings that it would be blown up. The British ignored the warnings and failed to evacuate the building. As a result, ninety-one people were killed, including fifteen Jews. The attack, like many others by the small, radical paramilitary groups, caused outrage among the British and consternation within the mainstream Jewish community, which condemned all such terrorist attacks.

When World War II ended, the British made it clear that they would not implement the Balfour Declaration. They also continued to severely restrict Jewish immigration, preventing the now stateless Jewish survivors of the Holocaust from going to their homeland. A number of ships carrying immigrants were turned back or sunk or their passengers arrested and imprisoned on Cyprus. The most famous case was that of the *Exodus*, a ship that left France July 11, 1947, carrying forty-five hundred immigrants. The British navy challenged and boarded the ship, killing three Jews. The immigrants were forcibly transported back to Germany in British ships.

The British people became increasingly distraught about

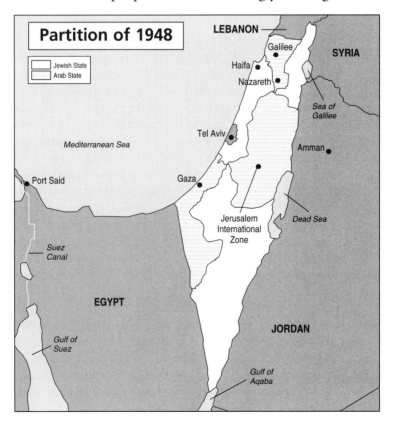

the events in Palestine, where mandatory authorities were unable to keep order. Arabs continued attacking the Jews, and now the Jews were increasingly fighting back. This had never particularly upset people in England because English citizens had remained largely above the fray; however, Jews were now increasingly attacking British targets. The Haganah had turned offensive but still was focusing on military targets. The militants, however, were humiliating and sometimes murdering British soldiers in response, they said, to what the British were doing to the Jews.

By February 1947 the British government had had enough and decided to turn the question of what to do with Palestine over to the United Nations (UN). The expectation was that the UN would fail to resolve the issue and leave it to the British to do what they wanted. At that point the British expected to be able to take whatever measures were necessary to pacify the country. The British tried to insure this outcome by specifying that the Jews and Arabs had to agree on any proposed solution—something they knew would be impossible.

As had occurred many times before, the UN sent a delegation, the UN Special Committee on Palestine (UNSCOP), to investigate the cause of the conflict between Jews and Arabs and listen to their respective positions. The majority of the delegates came to the same conclusion that the British Peel commission had arrived at almost exactly a decade earlier, namely, that the only fair way to resolve the dispute was to divide Palestine into both an Arab and Jewish state.

The UN adopted a resolution partitioning Palestine on November 29, 1947. The Arabs rejected the partition, insisting that they were entitled to all of Palestine, and subsequently went to war to prevent its implementation. Their publicly declared aim was to destroy the Jewish state. Since that date only two Arab states, Egypt and Jordan, have abandoned that goal and made peace with Israel. The other Arab states officially remain at war with Israel.

The Jews were also not enthusiastic about the partition resolution. They believed the Jewish homeland had already been partitioned once when the British created Transjordan. They were now being asked to accept statehood in an area a fraction of the size of the original Promised Land. Though they were offered about 60 percent of the territory of Palestine, most of that was the infertile land of the Negev desert region. Furthermore, the UN plan called for the internationalization of Jerusalem, which meant the Jews had to give up the place that had been their ancient capital and the focal point of their connection to the Holy Land for centuries. From a practical standpoint it meant the isolation of one hundred thousand Jews living in the city who were to be surrounded by the Arab state that was to encircle the internationalized area.

Despite what Zionists viewed as an unsatisfactory offer, they decided to accept the plan because it meant the establishment of a Jewish state with the backing of the international community. The Jews knew they would have to fight the Arabs to keep the area they had been allotted, but they believed that once the state was established they could build it and make it strong.

The conflict between Jews and Arabs did not begin or end with the founding of the state of Israel on May 14, 1948. Since then Israel has fought several wars with its neighbors and has experienced internal conflict as Palestinians in Israeli-occupied territories have engaged in violent uprisings. Because both sides fervently believe they have the right to call the disputed territory their home, the ongoing conflict has proven frustratingly resistant to international peacemaking efforts. Thus, over fifty years after its occurrence, the founding of the state of Israel remains a contentious event.

Chapter 1

Debating the Promise of a Jewish Homeland

1

The Jews Need a National Home in Palestine

Richard Gottheil

During the nineteenth century, a number of Jewish thinkers came to the conclusion that anti-Semitism was ineradicable and that the only hope of Jewish survival in the long run was the creation of a Jewish homeland. For most Jews, the only possible home for the Jews was the land of Israel, believed to have been promised by God, where the ancient Jewish nation had once flourished. The movement to establish a Jewish national home in Palestine was know as Zionism. In the following speech, originally delivered in November 1898, Richard Gottheil outlines the goals of Zionism. Gottheil argues that the assimilation of Jews in existing nations is not a practical goal due to the persistence of anti-Semitism. He concludes that the well-being of the Jewish people can only be guaranteed through the creation of a nation in their historic home of Palestine. Gottheil was a professor of Semitic languages and Rabbinical Literature at Columbia University in New York and president of the American Federation of Zionists.

I know that there are a great many of our people who look for a final solution of the Jewish question in what they call "assimilation." The more the Jews assimilate themselves to their surroundings, they think, the more completely will the causes for anti-Jewish feeling cease to exist. But have you ever for a moment stopped to consider what assimila-

Richard Gottheil, "The Aims of Zionism," speech, November 1, 1898, New York.

tion means? It has very pertinently been pointed out that the use of the word is borrowed from the dictionary of physiology. But in physiology it is not the food which assimilates itself into the body. It is the body which assimilates the food. The Jew may wish to be assimilated; he may do all he will towards this end. But if the great mass in which he lives does not wish to assimilate him—what then? If demands are made upon the Jew which practically mean extermination, which practically mean his total effacement from among the nations of the globe and from among the religious forces of the world,—what answer will you give? And the demands made are practically of that nature.

I can imagine it possible for a people who are possessed of an active and aggressive charity which it expresses, not only in words, but also in deeds, to contain and live at peace with men of the most varied habits. But, unfortunately, such people do not exist; nations are swayed by feelings which are dictated solely by their own self-interests; and the Zionists in meeting this state of things, are the most practical as well as the most ideal of the Jews.

There is no place where that which is distinctively Jewish in [the Jew's] manner or in his way of life is à la mode.

It is quite useless to tell the English workingman that his Jewish fellow-laborer from Russia has actually increased the riches of the United Kingdom; that he has created quite a new industry,—that of making ladies' cloaks, for which formerly England sent £2,000,000 to the continent every year. He sees in him some one who is different to himself, and unfortunately successful, though different. And until that difference entirely ceases, whether of habit, of way, or of religious observance, he will look upon him and treat him as an enemy.

An Especial Disadvantage

For the Jew has this especial disadvantage. There is no place where that which is distinctively Jewish in his manner or in his way of life is *à la mode*. We may well laugh at the Irishman's brogue; but in Ireland, he knows, his brogue is at home. We may poke fun at the Frenchman as he shrugs his shoulders and speaks with every member of his body. The Frenchman feels that in France it is the proper thing so to do. Even the Turk will wear his fez, and feel little the worse for the occasional jibes with which the street boy may greet it. But this consciousness, this ennobling consciousness, is all denied the Jew. What he does is nowhere *à la mode*; no, not even his features; and if he can disguise these by parting his hair in the middle or cutting his beard to a point, he feels he is on the road towards assimilation. He is even ready to use the term "Jewish" for what he considers uncouth and low.

We believe that [a Jewish national] home can only naturally . . . be found . . . in Palestine.

For such as these amongst us, Zionism also has its message. It wishes to give back to the Jew that nobleness of spirit, that confidence in himself, that belief in his own powers which only perfect freedom can give. With a home of his own, he will no longer feel himself a pariah among the nations, he will nowhere hide his own peculiarities,—peculiarities to which he has a right as much as any one,—but will see that those peculiarities carry with them a message which will force for them the admiration of the world. He will feel that he belongs somewhere and not everywhere. He will try to be something and not everything. The great word which Zionism preaches is conciliation of conflicting aims, of conflicting lines of action; conciliation of Jew to Jew. It means conciliation of the non-Jewish world to the Jew as well. It wishes to heal old wounds; and by frankly confessing differences which do exist, however much we try to explain them away, to work out its own salvation upon its own ground, and from these to send forth its spiritual message to a conciliated world.

But, you will ask, if Zionism is able to find a permanent home in Palestine for those Jews who are forced to go there as well as those who wish to go, what is to become of us who have entered, to such a degree, into the life around us, and who feel able to continue as we have begun? What is to be our relation to the new Jewish polity? I can only answer: Exactly the same as is the relation of people of other nationalities all the world over to their parent home. What becomes of the Englishman in every corner of the globe? What becomes of the German? Does the fact that the great mass of their people live in their own land prevent them from doing their whole duty towards the land in which they happen to live? Is the German-American considered less of an American because he cultivates the German language and is interested in the fate of his fellow-Germans at home? Is the Irish-American less of an American because he gathers money to help his struggling brethren in the Green Isle? Or are the Scandinavian-Americans less worthy of the title Americans, because they consider precious the bonds which bind them to the land of their birth, as well as those which bind them to the land of their adoption?

Nay! It would seem to me that just those who are so afraid that our action will be misinterpreted should be among the greatest helpers in the Zionist cause. For those who feel no racial and national communion with the life from which they have sprung should greet with joy the turning of Jewish immigration to some place other than the land in which they dwell. They must feel, for example, that a continual influx of Jews who are not Americans is a continual menace to the more or less complete absorption for which they are striving.

The Zionist Position

But I must not detain you much longer. Will you permit me to sum up for you the position which we Zionists take in the following statements:

We believe that the Jews are something more than a purely religious body; that they are not only a race, but also a nation; though a nation without as yet two important requisites—a common home and a common language.

We believe that if an end is to be made to Jewish misery and to the exceptional position which the Jews occupy,—which is the primary cause of Jewish misery,—the Jewish nation must be placed once again in a home of its own.

We believe that such a national regeneration is the fulfillment of the hope which has been present to the Jew throughout his long and painful history.

We believe that only by means of such a national regeneration can the religious regeneration of the Jews take place, and they be put in a position to do that work in the religious world which Providence has appointed for them.

We believe that such a home can only naturally, and

without violence to their whole past, be found in the land of their fathers—in Palestine.

We believe that such a return must have the guarantee of the great powers of the world in order to secure for the Jews a stable future.

And we hold that this does not mean that all Jews must return to Palestine.

This, ladies and gentlemen, is the Zionist program. Shall we be able to carry it through? I cannot believe that the Jewish people have been preserved throughout these centuries either for eternal misery or for total absorption at this stage of the world's history. I cannot think that our people have so far misunderstood their own purpose in life, as now to give the lie to their own past and to every hope which has animated their suffering body.

Bear with me but a few moments longer while I read the words which a Christian writer puts into the mouth of a Jew. "The effect of our separateness will not be completed and have its hightest transformation, unless our race takes on again the character of a nationality. That is the fulfillment of the religious trust that molded them into a people, whose life has made half the inspiration of the world. . . . Revive the organic centre; let the unity of Israel which has made the growth and form of its religion be an outward reality. Looking toward a land and a polity, our dispersed people in all the ends of the earth may share the dignity of a national life which has a voice among the peoples of the East and the West—which will plant the wisdom and skill of our race so that it may be, as of old, a medium of transmission and understanding. Let that come to pass, and the living warmth will spread to the weak extremities of Israel. Let the central fire be kindled again, and the light will reach afar. The degraded and scorned of the race will learn to think of their sacred land, not as a place for saintly beggary to await death in loathsome idleness, but as a republic, where the Jewish spirit manifests itself in a new order founded on the old, purified, enriched by the experiences which our greatest sons have gathered from the life of the ages. A new Judea, poised between East and West—a covenant of reconciliation. The sons of Judah have to choose, that God may again choose them. The Messianic time is the time when Israel shall will the planting of the national ensign. The divine principle of our race is action, choice, resolved memory. Let us help to will our own better future of the world—not renounce our higher gift and say: 'Let us be as if we were not among the populations,' but choose our full heritage, claim the brotherhood of our nation, and carry into it a new brotherhood with the nations of the Gentiles. The vision is there; it will be fulfilled."

These are the words of the non-Jewish Zionist, George Eliot. We take hope, for has not that Jewish Zionist said: "We belong to a race that can do everything but fail."

2

Early Promises of Arab Independence

Husayn ibn 'Ali and Henry McMahon

The central figure in the Arab nationalist movement at the time of World War I was Husayn ibn 'Ali, who was appointed by the Turkish Committee of Union and Progress to the position of Sherif of Mecca in 1908. As Sherif, Husayn was responsible for the custody of Islam's shrines in the Hejaz (later Saudi Arabia) and, consequently, was recognized as one of the Muslims' spiritual leaders. In July 1915, Husayn sent a letter to Sir Henry McMahon, Britain's High Commissioner for Egypt, informing him of the terms for Arab participation in the war against the Turks. The letters between Husayn and McMahon that followed, excerpted below, outlined the areas that Britain was prepared to cede to the Arabs in exchange for their assistance. The Husayn-McMahon correspondence conspicuously fails to mention Palestine. The British argued the omission had been intentional, thereby justifying their refusal to grant the Arabs independence in Palestine after the war. McMahon himself later said he had never promised that Palestine was included in the promises he made. Nevertheless, the Arabs held then, as now, that the letters constituted a promise of independence in Palestine for the Arabs.

Translation of a letter from Sherif Husayn of Mecca to Sir Henry McMahon, His Majesty's High Commissioner at Cairo, July 14, 1915

Whereas the whole of the Arab nation without any exception have decided in these last years to accom-

Henry McMahon and Husayn ibn 'Ali, "The Hussein-McMahon Correspondence," www.jewishvirtuallibrary.org, 1915–1916.

plish their freedom, and grasp the reins of their administration both in theory and practice; and whereas they have found and felt that it is in the interest of the Government of Great Britain to support them and aid them in the attainment of their firm and lawful intentions (which are based upon the maintenance of the honour and dignity of their life) without any ulterior motives whatsoever unconnected with this object;

And whereas it is to their (the Arabs') interest also to prefer the assistance of the Government of Great Britain in consideration of their geographic position and economic interests, and also of the attitude of the above-mentioned Government, which is known to both nations and therefore need not be emphasized;

Subject to the above modifications, Great Britain is prepared to recognize and support the independence of the Arabs.

For these reasons the Arab nation sees fit to limit themselves, as time is short, to asking the Government of Great Britain, if it should think fit, for the approval, through her deputy or representative, of the following fundamental propositions, leaving out all things considered secondary in comparison with these, so that it may prepare all means necessary for attaining this noble purpose, until such time as it finds occasion for making the actual negotiations;

Firstly—England will acknowledge the independence of the Arab countries, bounded on the north by Mersina and Adana up to the 37th degree of latitude, on which degree fall Birijik, Urfa, Mardin, Midiat, Jezirat (Ibn 'Umar), Amadia, up to the border of Persia; on the east by the borders of Persia up to the Gulf of Basra; on the south by the Indian Ocean, with the exception of the position of Aden to remain as it is; on the west by the Red Sea, the Mediterranean Sea up to Mersina. England to approve the proclamation of an Arab Khalifate of Islam.

Secondly—The Arab Government of the Sherif will acknowledge that England shall have the preference in all economic enterprises in the Arab countries whenever conditions of enterprises are otherwise equal.

Thirdly—For the security of this Arab independence

and the certainty of such preference of economic enterprises, both high contracting parties will offer mutual assistance, to the best ability of their military and naval forces, to
face any foreign Power which may attack either party. Peace
not to be decided without agreement of both parties.

Fourthly—If one of the parties enters into an aggressive
conflict, the other party will assume a neutral attitude, and
in case of such party wishing the other to join forces, both
to meet and discuss the conditions.

Fifthly—England will acknowledge the abolition of foreign privileges in the Arab countries, and will assist the
Government of the Sherif in an International Convention
for confirming such abolition.

Sixthly—Articles 3 and 4 of this treaty will remain in
vigour for fifteen years, and, if either wishes it to be re-
newed, one year's notice before lapse of treaty is to be given.

Consequently, and as the whole of the Arab nation have
(praise be to God) agreed and united for the attainment, at
all costs and finally, of this noble object, they beg the Government of Great Britain to answer them positively or neg-
atively in a period of thirty days after receiving this intima-
tion; and if this period should lapse before they receive an
answer, they reserve to themselves complete freedom of action. Moreover, we (the Sherif's family) will consider ourselves free in work and deed from the bonds of our previous
declaration which we made through Ali Effendi.

Translation of a letter from McMahon to Husayn, August 30, 1915

To his Highness the Sherif Hussein.

(After compliments and salutations.)

We have the honour to thank you for your frank expressions of the sincerity of your feeling towards England.
We rejoice, moreover, that your Highness and your people
are of one opinion—that Arab interests are English interests
and English Arab. To this intent we confirm to you the
terms of Lord [Horatio] Kitchener's [British Secretary of
War] message, which reached you by the hand of Ali Effendi, and in which was stated clearly our desire for the independence of Arabia and its inhabitants, together with our
approval of the Arab Khalifate when it should be proclaimed. We declare once more that His Majesty's Government would welcome the resumption of the Khalifate by an

Arab of true race. With regard to the questions of limits and boundaries, it would appear to be premature to consume our time in discussing such details in the heat of war, and while, in many portions of them, the Turk is up to now in effective occupation; especially as we have learned, with surprise and regret, that some of the Arabs in those very parts, far from assisting us, are neglecting this their supreme opportunity and are lending their arms to the German and the Turk, to the new despoiler and the old oppressor. . . .

Friendly reassurances. Salutations!

(Signed) A.H. McMAHON.

Translation of a letter from Husayn to McMahon, September 9, 1915

To his Excellency the Most Exalted, the Most Eminent—the British High Commissioner in Egypt; may God grant him Success.

With great cheerfulness and delight I received your letter dated the 19th Shawal, 1333 (the 30th August, 1915), and have given it great consideration and regard, in spite of the impression I received from it of ambiguity and its tone of coldness and hesitation with regard to our essential point.

It is necessary to make clear to your Excellency our sincerity towards the illustrious British Empire and our confession of preference for it in all cases and matters and under all forms and circumstances. The real interests of the followers of our religion necessitate this.

Nevertheless, your Excellency will pardon me and permit me to say clearly that the coolness and hesitation which you have displayed in the question of the limits and boundaries by saying that the discussion of these at present is of no use and is a loss of time, and that they are still in the hands of the Government which is ruling them, &c., might be taken to infer an estrangement or something of the sort.

As the limits and boundaries demanded are not those of one person whom we should satisfy and with whom we should discuss them after the war is over, but our peoples have seen that the life of their new proposal is bound at least by these limits and their word is united on this.

Therefore, they have found it necessary first to discuss this point with the Power in whom they now have their confidence and trust as a final appeal, viz., the illustrious British Empire.

Their reason for this union and confidence is mutual interest, the necessity of regulating territorial divisions and the feelings of their inhabitants, so that they may know how to base their future and life, so not to meet her (England?) or any of her Allies in opposition to their resolution which would produce a contrary issue, which God forbid.

For the object is, honourable Minister, the truth which is established on a basis which guarantees the essential sources of life in future.

Yet within these limits they have not included places inhabited by a foreign race. It is a vain show of words and titles.

May God have mercy on the Khalifate and comfort Moslems in it.

I am confident that your Excellency will not doubt that it is not I personally who am demanding of these limits which include only our race, but that they are all proposals of the people, who, in short, believe that they are necessary for economic life.

Is this not right, your Excellency the Minister?

In a word, your high Excellency, we are firm in our sincerity and declaring our preference for loyalty towards you, whether you are satisfied with us, as has been said, or angry.

With reference to your remark in your letter above mentioned that some of our people are still doing their utmost in promoting the interests of Turkey, your goodness (lit. "perfectness") would not permit you to make this an excuse for the tone of coldness and hesitation with regard to our demands, demands which I cannot admit that you, as a man of sound opinion, will deny to be necessary for our existence; nay, they are the essential essence of our life, material and moral.

Up to the present moment I am myself with all my might carrying out in my country all things in conformity with the Islamic law, all things which tend to benefit the rest of the Kingdom, and I shall continue to do so until it pleases God to order otherwise.

In order to reassure your Excellency I can declare that the whole country, together with those who you say are submitting themselves to Turco-German orders, are all waiting the result of these negotiations, which are dependent only on your refusal or acceptance of the question of the limits and on your declaration of safeguarding their religion first and then the rest of rights from any harm or danger.

Whatever the illustrious Government of Great Britain finds conformable to its policy on this subject, communicate it to us and specify to us the course we should follow. . . .

Translation of a letter from McMahon to Husayn, October 24, 1915

I have received your letter of the 29th Shawal, 1333, with much pleasure and your expressions of friendliness and sincerity have given me the greatest satisfaction.

I regret that you should have received from my last letter the impression that I regarded the question of the limits and boundaries with coldness and hesitation; such was not the case, but it appeared to me that the time had not yet come when that question could be discussed in a conclusive manner.

I have realised, however, from your last letter that you regard this question as one of vital and urgent importance. I have, therefore, lost no time in informing the Government of Great Britain of the contents of your letter, and it is with great pleasure that I communicate to you on their behalf the following statement, which I am confident you will receive with satisfaction:

The two districts of Mersina and Alexandretta and portions of Syria lying to the west of the districts of Damascus, Homs, Hama and Aleppo cannot be said to be purely Arab, and should be excluded from the limits demanded.

With the above modification, and without prejudice of our existing treaties with Arab chiefs, we accept those limits.

As for those regions lying within those frontiers wherein Great Britain is free to act without detriment to the interest of her ally, France, I am empowered in the name of the Government of Great Britain to give the following assurances and make the following reply to your letter:

1. Subject to the above modifications, Great Britain is prepared to recognize and support the independence of the Arabs in all the regions within the limits demanded by the Sherif of Mecca.

2. Great Britain will guarantee the Holy Places against all external aggression and will recognise their inviolability.

3. When the situation admits, Great Britain will give to the Arabs her advice and will assist them to establish what may appear to be the most suitable forms of government in those various territories.

4. On the other hand, it is understood that the Arabs have decided to seek the advice and guidance of Great Britain only, and that such European advisers and officials as may be required for the formation of a sound form of administration will be British.

5. With regard to the vilayets of Bagdad and Basra, the Arabs will recognise that the established position and interests of Great Britain necessitate special administrative arrangements in order to secure these territories from foreign aggression, to promote the welfare of the local populations and to safeguard our mutual economic interests.

I am convinced that this declaration will assure you beyond all possible doubt of the sympathy of Great Britain towards the aspirations of her friends the Arabs and will result in a firm and lasting alliance, the immediate results of which will be the expulsion of the Turks from the Arab countries and the freeing of the Arab peoples from the Turkish yoke, which for so many years has pressed heavily upon them. . . .

(Signed) A.H. McMAHON.

Translation of a letter from Husayn to McMahon, November 5, 1915

I received with great pleasure your honoured letter, dated the 15th Zil Hijja (the 24th October, 1915), to which I beg to answer as follows:

1. In order to facilitate an agreement and to render a service to Islam, and at the same time to avoid all that may cause Islam troubles and hardships—seeing moreover that we have great consideration for the distinguished qualities and dispositions of the Government of Great Britain—we renounce our insistence on the inclusion of the vilayets of Mersina and Adana in the Arab Kingdom. But the two vilayets of Aleppo and Beirut and their sea coasts are purely Arab vilayets, and there is no difference between a Moslem and a Christian Arab: they are both descendants of one forefather.

We Moslems will follow the footsteps of the Commander of the Faithful Omar ibn Khattab, and other Khalifs succeeding him, who ordained in the laws of the Moslem Faith that Moslems should treat the Christians as they treat themselves. He, Omar, declared with reference to Christians: "They will have the same privileges and submit to the same duties as ourselves." They will thus enjoy their civic rights in as much as it accords with the general interests of the whole nation.

2. As the Iraqi vilayets are parts of the pure Arab Kingdom, and were in fact the seat of its Government in the time of Ali ibn Abu Talib, and in the time of all the Khalifs who succeeded him; and as in them began the civilisation of the Arabs, and as their towns were the first towns built in Islam where the Arab power became so great; therefore they are greatly valued by all Arabs far and near, and their traditions cannot be forgotten by them. Consequently, we cannot satisfy the Arab nations or make them submit to give us such a title to nobility. But in order to render an accord easy, and taking into consideration the assurances mentioned in the fifth article of your letter to keep and guard our mutual interests in that country as they are one and the same, for all these reasons we might agree to leave under the British administration for a short time those districts now occupied by the British troops without the rights of either party being prejudiced thereby (especially those of the Arab nation; which interests are to it economic and vital), and against a suitable sum paid as compensation to the Arab Kingdom for the period of occupation, in order to meet the expenses which every new kingdom is bound to support; at the same time respecting your agreements with the Sheikhs of those districts, and especially those which are essential.

When the Arabs know the Government of Great Britain is their ally . . . , then to enter the war at once will . . . be in conformity with the general interest of the Arabs.

---

3. In your desire to hasten the movement we see not only advantages, but grounds of apprehension. The first of these grounds is the fear of the blame of the Moslems of the opposite party (as has already happened in the past), who would declare that we have revolted against Islam and ruined its forces. The second is that, standing in the face of Turkey which is supported by all the forces of Germany, we do not know what Great Britain and her Allies would do if one of the Entente Powers were weakened and obliged to make peace. We fear that the Arab nation will then be left

alone in the face of Turkey together with her allies, but we would not at all mind if we were to face the Turks alone. Therefore it is necessary to take these points into consideration in order to avoid a peace being concluded in which the parties concerned may decide the fate of our people as if we had taken part in the war without making good our claims to official consideration.

4. The Arab nation has a strong belief that after this war is over the Turks under German influence will direct their efforts to provoke the Arabs and violate their rights, both material and moral, to wipe out their nobility and honour and reduce them to utter submission as they are determined to ruin them entirely. The reasons for the slowness shown in our action have already been stated.

5. When the Arabs know the Government of Great Britain is their ally who will not leave them to themselves at the conclusion of peace in the face of Turkey and Germany, and that she will support and will effectively defend them, then to enter the war at once will, no doubt, be in conformity with the general interest of the Arabs. . . .

Translation of a letter from McMahon to Husayn, December 14, 1915

(After customary greetings and acknowledgment of previous letter.)

I am gratified to observe that you agree to the exclusion of the districts of Mersina and Adana from boundaries of the Arab territories.

I also note with great pleasure and satisfaction your assurances that the Arabs are determined to act in conformity with the precepts laid down by Omar Ibn Khattab and the early Khalifs, which secure the rights and privileges of all religions alike.

In stating that the Arabs are ready to recognise and respect all our treaties with Arab chiefs, it is, of course, understood that this will apply to all territories included in the Arab Kingdom, as the Government of Great Britain cannot repudiate engagements which already exist.

With regard to the vilayets of Aleppo and Beirut, the Government of Great Britain have fully understood and taken careful note of your observations, but, as the interests of our ally, France, are involved in them both, the question will require careful consideration and a further communication on the subject will be addressed to you in due course.

The Government of Great Britain, as I have already informed you, are ready to give all guarantees of assistance and support within their power to the Arab Kingdom, but their interests demand, as you yourself have recognised, a friendly and stable administration in the vilayet of Bagdad, and the adequate safeguarding of these interests calls for a much fuller and more detailed consideration than the present situation and the urgency of these negotiations permit.

We fully appreciate your desire for caution, and have no wish to urge you to hasty action, which might jeopardise the eventual success of your projects, but, in the meantime, it is most essential that you should spare no effort to attach all the Arab peoples to our united cause and urge them to afford no assistance to our enemies.

It is on the success of these efforts and on the more active measures which the Arabs may hereafter take in support of our cause, when the time for action comes, that the permanence and strength of our agreement must depend.

Under these circumstances I am further directed by the Government of Great Britain to inform you that you may rest assured that Great Britain has no intention of concluding any peace in terms of which the freedom of the Arab peoples from German and Turkish domination does not form an essential condition.

As an earnest of our intentions, and in order to aid you in your efforts in our joint cause, I am sending you by your trustworthy messenger a sum of twenty thousand pounds.

(Customary ending.)

(Signed) H. McMAHON.

Translation of a letter from Husayn to McMahon, January 1, 1916

We received from the bearer your letter, dated the 9th Safar (the 14th December, 1915), with great respect and honour, and I have understood its contents, which caused me the greatest pleasure and satisfaction, as it removed that which had made me uneasy. . . .

As regards the northern parts and their coasts, we have already stated in our previous letter what were the utmost possible modifications, and all this was only done so to fulfill those aspirations whose attainment is desired by the will of the Blessed and Supreme God. It is this same feeling and desire which impelled us to avoid what may possibly injure the alliance of Great Britain and France and the agreement made between them during the present wars and calamities; yet we find it our duty that the eminent minister should be sure that, at the first opportunity after this war is finished, we shall ask you (what we avert our eyes from today) for what we now leave to France in Beirut and its coasts.

I do not find it necessary to draw your attention to the fact that our plan is of greater security to the interests and protection of the rights of Great Britain than it is to us, and will necessarily be so whatever may happen, so that Great Britain may finally see her friends in that contentment and advancement which she is endeavouring to establish for them now, especially as her Allies being neighbours to us will be the germ of difficulties and discussion with which there will be no peaceful conditions. In addition to which the citizens of Beirut will decidedly never accept such dismemberment, and they may oblige us to undertake new measures which may exercise Great Britain, certainly not less than her present troubles, because of our belief and certainty in the reciprocity and indeed the identity of our interests, which is the only cause that caused us never to care to negotiate with any other Power but you. Consequently, it is impossible to allow any derogation that gives France, or any other Power, a span of land in those regions.

I declare this, and I have a strong belief, which the living will inherit from the dead, in the declarations which you give in the conclusion of your honoured letter. Therefore, the honourable and eminent Minister should believe and be sure, together with Great Britain, that we still remain firm to our resolution which [British administrator Ronald] Storrs learnt from us two years ago, for which we await the opportunity suitable to our situation, especially in view of that action the time of which has now come near and which destiny drives towards us with great haste and clearness, so that we and those who are of our opinion may have reasons for such action against any criticisms or responsibilities imposed upon us in future.

Your expression "we do not want to push you to any hasty action which might jeopardise the success of your aim" does not need any more explanation except what we may ask for, when necessary, such as arms, ammunition, &c.

I deem this sufficient, as I have occupied much of your

Honour's time. I beg to offer you my great veneration and respect.

Translation of a letter from McMahon to Husayn, January 25, 1916

We fully realise and entirely appreciate the motives which guide you in this important question, and we know well that you are acting entirely in the interests of the Arab peoples and with no thought beyond their welfare.

We take note of your remarks concerning the vilayet of Baghdad, and will take the question into careful consideration when the enemy has been defeated and the time for peaceful settlement arrives.

As regards the northern parts, we note with satisfaction your desire to avoid anything which might possibly injure the alliance of Great Britain and France. It is, as you know, our fixed determination that nothing shall be permitted to interfere in the slightest degree with our united prosecution of this war to a victorious conclusion. Moreover, when the victory has been won, the friendship of Great Britain and France will become yet more firm and enduring, cemented by the blood of Englishmen and Frenchmen who have died side by side fighting for the cause of right and liberty.

In this great cause Arabia is now associated, and God grant that the result of our mutual efforts and co-operation will bind us in a lasting friendship to the mutual welfare and happiness of us all.

We are greatly pleased to hear of the action you are taking to win all the Arabs over to our joint cause, and to dissuade them from giving any assistance to our enemies, and we leave it to your discretion to seize the most favourable moment for further and more decided measures.

3

The British Promise a Home for the Jews in Palestine

Arthur James Balfour

During World War I the British believed that supporting the Zionist program would win them the gratitude of American Jews, who would then lobby their government to join Britain in the war. (The United States ultimately did join the war effort, though the Jews had little to do with the U.S. decision.) In 1917, the British declared their support for a Jewish homeland in the form of a letter from Lord Arthur James Balfour to Baron Edmond de Rothschild, the unofficial leader of British Jewry. This text became known as the Balfour Declaration. For the next forty years, the Zionists would fight for the implementation of the declaration.

Foreign Office
November 2nd, 1917
Dear Lord Rothschild,

I have much pleasure in conveying to you, on behalf of His Majesty's Government, the following declaration of sympathy with Jewish Zionist aspirations which has been submitted to, and approved by, the Cabinet.

"His Majesty's Government view with favour the establishment in Palestine of a national home for the Jewish people, and will use their best endeavours to facilitate the achievement of this object, it being clearly understood that nothing shall be done which may prejudice the civil and re-

Arthur James Balfour, "The Balfour Declaration," www.mfa.gov.il, Israel Ministry of Foreign Affairs, 1917.

ligious rights of existing non-Jewish communities in Palestine, or the rights and political status enjoyed by Jews in any other country."

I should be grateful if you would bring this declaration to the knowledge of the Zionist Federation.

Yours sincerely,
Arthur James Balfour

4

Palestine Should Not Become a Jewish State

Inter-Allied Commission on Mandates in Turkey

Following the peace process at the end of World War I, U.S. president Woodrow Wilson decided to send an Inter-Allied Commission on Mandates in Turkey to the former Turkish (Ottoman) empire to determine what type of political arrangement the inhabitants preferred. Due to French and British opposition, the commission ultimately consisted of only two people—the Americans Henry C. King and Charles R. Crane. As part of their report, known as the King-Crane Report, the authors weigh in against following the extreme Zionist program to create an independent Jewish state in Palestine. King and Crane insist that the creation of such a state would violate the civil and religious rights of the non-Jewish inhabitants of the region, who are overwhelmingly opposed to the Zionist program.

W e recommend . . . serious modification of the extreme Zionist Program for Palestine of unlimited immigration of Jews, looking finally to making Palestine distinctly a Jewish State.

(1) The Commissioners began their study of Zionism with minds predisposed in its favor, but the actual facts in Palestine, coupled with the force of the general principles proclaimed by the Allies and accepted by the Syrians, have driven them to the recommendation here made.

(2) The Commission was abundantly supplied with literature on the Zionist program by the Zionist Commission

Inter-Allied Commission on Mandates in Turkey, "Recommendations of the King-Crane Commission on Syria and Palestine," www.jewishvirtuallibrary.org, August 28, 1919.

to Palestine; heard in conferences much concerning the Zionist colonies and their claims; and personally saw something of what had been accomplished. They found much to approve in the aspirations and plans of the Zionists, and had warm appreciation for the devotion of many of the colonists, and for their success, by modern methods, in overcoming great natural obstacles.

The non-Jewish population of Palestine—nearly nine-tenths of the whole—are emphatically against the entire Zionist program.

---

(3) The Commission recognized also that definite encouragement had been given to the Zionists by the Allies in Mr. Balfour's often quoted statement, in its approval by other representatives of the Allies. If, however, the strict terms of the Balfour Statement are adhered to—favoring "the establishment in Palestine of a national home for the Jewish people, it being clearly understood that nothing shall be done which may prejudice the civil and religious rights of existing non-Jewish communities in Palestine"—it can hardly be doubted that the extreme Zionist Program must be greatly modified. For a "national home for the Jewish people" is not equivalent to making Palestine into a Jewish State; nor can the erection of such a Jewish State be accomplished without the gravest trespass upon the "civil and religious rights of existing non-Jewish communities in Palestine." The fact came out repeatedly in the Commission's conference with Jewish representatives, that the Zionists looked forward to a practically complete dispossession of the present non-Jewish inhabitants of Palestine, by various forms of purchase.

Wilson's Principles

In his address of July 4, 1918, President Wilson laid down the following principle as one of the four great "ends for which the associated peoples of the world were fighting": "The settlement of every question, whether of territory, of sovereignty, of economic arrangement or of political relationship upon the basis of the free acceptance of that settlement by the people immediately concerned, and not upon the basis of the material interest or advantage of any other nation or people which may desire a different settlement for the sake of its own exterior influence or mastery." If that principle is to rule, and so the wishes of Palestine's population are to be decisive as to what is to be done with Palestine, then it is to be remembered that the non-Jewish population of Palestine—nearly nine-tenths of the whole—are emphatically against the entire Zionist program. There was no one thing upon which the population of Palestine was more agreed than upon this. To subject a people so minded to unlimited Jewish immigration, and to steady financial and social pressure to surrender the land, would be a gross violation of the principle just quoted, and of the peoples' rights, though it kept within the forms of law.

It is to be noted also that the feeling against the Zionist program is not confined to Palestine, but shared very generally by the people throughout Syria, as our conferences clearly showed. More than 72 per cent—1350 in all—of all the petitions in the whole of Syria were directed against the Zionist program. Only two requests—those for a united Syria and for independence—had a larger support. This general feeling was only voiced by the "General Syrian Congress," in the seventh, eighth and tenth resolutions of their statement.

Intense Anti-Zionism

The Peace Conference should not shut its eyes to the fact that the anti-Zionist feeling in Palestine and Syria is intense and not lightly to be flouted. No British officer, consulted by the Commissioners, believed that the Zionist program could be carried out except by force of arms. The officers generally thought a force of not less than fifty thousand soldiers would be required even to initiate the program. That of itself is evidence of a strong sense of the injustice of the Zionist program, on the part of the non-Jewish populations of Palestine and Syria. Decisions, requiring armies to carry out, are sometimes necessary, but they are surely not gratuitously to be taken in the interests of a serious injustice. For the initial claim, often submitted by Zionist representatives, that they have a "right" to Palestine, based on an occupation of two thousand years ago, can hardly be seriously considered.

There is a further consideration that cannot justly be ignored, if the world is to look forward to Palestine becoming a definitely Jewish state, however gradually that may take place. That consideration grows out of the fact that Palestine is "the Holy Land" for Jews, Christians, and Moslems alike. Millions of Christians and Moslems all over the world are quite as much concerned as the Jews with conditions in Palestine, especially with those conditions which touch upon religious feeling and rights. The relations in these matters in Palestine are most delicate and difficult. With the best possible intentions, it may be doubted whether the Jews could possibly seem to either Christians or Moslems proper guardians of the holy places, or custodians of the Holy Land as a whole. The reason is this: the places which are most sacred to Christians—those having to do with Jesus—and which are also sacred to Moslems, are not only not sacred to Jews, but abhorrent to them. It is simply impossible, under those circumstances, for Moslems and Christians to feel satisfied to have these places in Jewish hands, or under the custody of Jews. There are still other places about which Moslems must have the same feeling. In fact, from this point of view, the Moslems, just because the sacred places of all three religions are sacred to them, have made very naturally much more satisfactory custodians of the holy places than the Jews could be. It must be believed that the precise meaning, in this respect, of the complete Jewish occupation of Palestine has not been fully sensed by those who urge the extreme Zionist program. For it would intensify, with a certainty like fate, the anti-Jewish feeling both in Palestine and in all other portions of the world which look to Palestine as "the Holy Land."

The Commissioners feel bound to recommend that only a greatly reduced Zionist program be attempted.

In view of all these considerations, and with a deep sense of sympathy for the Jewish cause, the Commissioners feel bound to recommend that only a greatly reduced Zionist program be attempted by the Peace Conference, and even that, only very gradually initiated. This would have to mean that Jewish immigration should be definitely limited, and that the project for making Palestine distinctly a Jewish commonwealth should be given up.

There would then be no reason why Palestine could not

be included in a united Syrian State, just as other portions of the country, the holy places being cared for by an International and Inter-religious Commission, somewhat as at present, under the oversight and approval of the Mandatory and of the League of Nations. The Jews, of course, would have representation upon this Commission.

5

A Jewish State Will Hurt the Arabs

King Abdallah of Jordan

In 1921, Winston Churchill decided to reward one of the key Arab leaders who helped Britain defeat the Ottoman Turks in World War I, by taking nearly 80 percent of Palestine and creating an entirely new country and making their ally its king. This is how Transjordan, later Jordan, came into being. Abdallah, the Arab leader who was installed as the monarch, had a keen interest in the debate over what would happen to the remaining parts of Palestine, which he coveted for his kingdom. Ultimately, during the war of 1948, his army would take control of most of what was to be the Arab state under the partition resolution. However, in 1934, long before his forces invaded the newly formed state of Israel, the king wrote to Sir Arthur Wauchope, who was the British government's representative in the kingdom, to express his concerns about how the Balfour Declaration and the immigration of Jews to Palestine was affecting the Arabs.

---

1. I understand from His Excellency the Colonial Secretary that His Majesty's Government has placed complete trust in the person of Your Excellency and that you are the sole authority upon which it relies in the Palestine question. Appreciating as I do the gravity of this responsibility I cannot conceal my pleasure at this news because of my confidence in the good understanding and firm bonds of friendship that exist between your honourable person and myself. I am aware also that you have an unfettered love of justice

King Abdallah of Jordan, *My Memoirs Completed*, translated by Harold W. Glidden. London: Longman, 1978. Copyright © 1978 by Longman Group, Ltd. Reproduced by permission.

and a genuine discrimination for those things which link the interests of your noble government and people with the Arabs as opposed to others in the Near East.

With regard to the idea prevalent among us Arabs that the Jews in Great Britain enjoy a privileged position because some of their leaders occupy high posts in the government and in the House of Commons and thus are able to direct British policy along lines completely favourable to their own people rather than to others, I have learned also from His Excellency the Colonial Secretary[1] that this is not the case and that it is an erroneous belief. He has reassured me that on the contrary the British Government is not so influenced and that it follows a just course of action and one which is in accord with its national traditions.

For this and other reasons which I have already set forth I have deemed it fitting to write to Your Excellency on the subject of the Arab cause in Palestine, since any further delay would be reckoned as a grave disregard on my part of the national right of both the Arabs and their British friends.

2. The Arabs are greatly distressed because they perceive no concrete results from the reports of the British missions which in past years have been sent to Palestine to inquire into the true state of affairs there. This is in spite of the importance of their testimony and despite the truths contained in the White Paper[2] issued by former Colonial Secretary Lord Passfield.

Promises to Arabs Came First

3. The promises made to the Arabs during the World War were anterior to and more precise than the Balfour Declaration. It was these promises which moved a great many Palestinians—soldiers, officers, and civilians—to desert from the Turkish Army and rally to the banner of my father King Husayn in the Arab Revolt, during which its heroes fought side by side with the British forces. At that time the Zionists had absolutely no political position in Palestine and in no way constituted an element of its population.

4. The joint declaration issued in November 1918 by the two allied powers of Great Britain and France specifically stated that the Arabs would not be compelled to accept any

1. This probably refers to Sir Philip Cunliffe-Lister, who was Colonial Secretary from 9 November 1931 to 6 June 1935.   2. This was issued in 1930 as the result of an investigation into the causes of the disturbances of 1929.

form of government not agreeable to them. On the contrary, it was said that they would encourage the establishment of Arab national governments and that they would extend to them the assistance necessary for their consolidation and success. This declaration should be granted the importance it deserves and it should be taken into account when considering the carrying-out of the Balfour Declaration in Palestine.

The Arabs . . . see a manifest threat to their existence in the steady Jewish immigration into Palestine.

---

5. The Balfour Declaration provides that the Jews should have a national home in Palestine. The indications, however, are that *the Jews by various means and without opposition have been able to devise a programme for turning all of Palestine into a national home for the Jews.* If any impartial observer were to compare their position at the beginning of the immigration into Palestine with the great progress they have made up to the present in colonizing the country, *he would say that their success has been almost complete and that they will attain their goal in a few years.*

6. The Balfour Declaration lays down the condition that the interests of the Arab inhabitants are not to be harmed; in other words, that the interests of the Arabs are to be protected in their entirety. The Arabs, however, see a manifest threat to their existence in the steady Jewish immigration into Palestine accompanied by an influx of illegal arrivals in flagrant violation of this promise. In addition, the fears of the Arab political leaders are supported by the fact that the sale of land continues unrestricted and every day one piece of land after another is torn from the hands of the Arabs.

I know that this cannot be completely stopped even by the use of force. Nevertheless, I draw Your Excellency's attention to the difficult situation in which the Arabs find themselves in the face of the strong organization of the Zionists. In such cases it would be governments which would prevent the disappearance and submerging of a people. If these people possessed representatives in parliamentary or legislative bodies, they would be able to play their part in defending the people and countering the danger that threatens them.

7. Protection of the weak was one of the most honourable of the high aims for which the last World War was fought. What is more worthy of this noble principle than to remember it in times of peace in connection with the situation of the Palestine Arabs who made sacrifices in the war at a time when they were masters of their own country and without rivals for control of it?

Jews Bring Trouble

8. The Jewish immigration has brought to Palestine incompatible peoples of different principles and outlook from the Arabs, who have brought continual unrest and trouble to this peaceful and holy land. *Furthermore, Palestine has become a potential source of social danger the enormity of which will become apparent as soon as world peace is again disturbed;* this corruption will spread to the Arab countries in particular and to the Near East in general. I do not believe that the Government of Palestine would come to any different conclusion if it were to make a profound study of the situation; this is supported by the nature of certain clandestine Jewish groups the existence of which has been revealed by the law-courts.

The Jews have attempted and continue to attempt to go beyond the promises made in the Balfour Declaration.

---

9. The Jews have attempted and continue to attempt to go beyond the promises made in the Balfour Declaration and thereby have given rise in the minds of the Arabs to a fixed idea that *a Jewish state is being created which is masquerading under the name of the National Home.* The implications of this are causing fears to spread to the Arab countries outside of Palestine and to those persons in these countries who are in positions of important responsibility. The Jews have never given the slightest indication of their ability to amalgamate with the original Arab inhabitants of the country. I wish from the bottom of my heart that it were otherwise.

10. My experience leads me to believe that if the situation continues as it is, with unrestricted immigration and other things complained of by the Arabs, *it will lead to evil and terrible results in the near future.* I do not feel that at present sufficient thought is being given to this possibility; matters

are being dealt with on a day-to-day basis. As a result of this it is still said that there is room for new immigrants and that there is land which can be sold. Nevertheless, I hope that Your Excellency will join me in giving thought to the future we may face, and to the problems that may be most difficult to solve if immigration and the sale of land continue.

Your Excellency:

I lay before Your Excellency these matters which have disturbed the Arabs both in and out of Palestine. If I have told Your Excellency that the Muslim world is likewise disturbed by these events it is because I am quite certain that this is so. For this reason I have thought that I should draw Your Excellency's attention to these knotty problems which, with God's permission, I trust will be overcome by you.

I do not deny that Great Britain's interests have expanded in Palestine and the Arab countries since the war. But do you not feel, as I do, that in view of all this the continuation of the genuine friendship which the Arabs feel for your noble nation is an essential thing that must be nurtured and preserved?

Both in the past and in the present I have done all in my power to support these ties between the two nations. This is because I firmly believe that it is in the interest of the Arabs as well as the English to do so. I do not deny that my Arab people in Palestine have fallen into a number of political errors, but in my opinion this is all due to their overwhelming fear that their existence is being threatened. It is not to be expected, of course, that a people who are in such a state should preserve their normal balanced frame of mind or think as calmly as they ought to. For this reason their mistakes should be overlooked since the reasons for them are all too apparent.

I communicate to you in all frankness the fears of my Arab people in Palestine and I have summed them up in this memorandum to the best of my ability. It is my hope that you will consider this as an assistance from me to Your Excellency in the performance of the difficult duty which you have undertaken and will see it as motivated by sincere friendship for both my Arab people and my British friends.

Accept, Excellency, my highest esteem and my best greetings.

Your Excellency's sincere friend, 'Abdallah
Amman, 25 July 1934.

6

Britain Does Not Support a Jewish State in Palestine

British Government

In 1937, in response to Arab rioting, the British formed a commission to investigate the causes of the violence and formulate a possible resolution to the conflict between Jews and Arabs. The Peel Commission came to essentially the same conclusion the UN would a decade later; that is, the fairest solution would be to divide Palestine into two states, one Jewish and one Arab. Two years later, the British government issued a white paper that rejected the Peel Commission's partition plan on the grounds that it was not feasible. Instead, the government now proposed an independent state that would essentially be an Arab one, since it gave the Arabs veto power over Jewish immigration. The white paper was a complete repudiation of the Balfour Declaration and therefore vehemently opposed by the Zionists, who, from that point on, realized they could not rely on the British to support their national ambitions. The Arabs rejected the plan as well.

In the statement on Palestine, issued on 9 November, 1938, His Majesty's Government [Britain] announced their intention to invite representatives of the Arabs of Palestine, of certain neighboring countries and of the Jewish Agency to confer with them in London regarding future policy. It was their sincere hope that, as a result of full, free and frank discussions, some understanding might be

British Government, "British White Paper, 1939," www.yale.edu, June 1939.

reached. Conferences recently took place with Arab and Jewish delegations, lasting for a period of several weeks, and served the purpose of a complete exchange of views between British Ministers and the Arab and Jewish representatives. In the light of the discussions as well as of the situation in Palestine and of the Reports of the Royal Commission and the Partition Commission, certain proposals were formulated by His Majesty's Government and were laid before the Arab and Jewish delegations as the basis of an agreed settlement. Neither the Arab nor the Jewish delegation felt able to accept these proposals, and the conferences therefore did not result in an agreement. Accordingly His Majesty's Government are free to formulate their own policy, and after careful consideration they have decided to adhere generally to the proposals which were finally submitted to and discussed with the Arab and Jewish delegations.

The framers of the Mandate . . . could not have intended that Palestine should be converted into a Jewish state against the will of the Arab population.

The Mandate for Palestine, the terms of which were confirmed by the Council of the League of Nations in 1922, has governed the policy of successive British Governments for nearly 20 years. It embodies the Balfour Declaration and imposes on the Mandatory four main obligations. These obligations are set out in Article 2, 6 and 13 of the Mandate. There is no dispute regarding the interpretation of one of these obligations, that touching the protection of and access to the Holy Places and religious buildings or sites. The other three main obligations are generally as follows:

To place the country under such political, administrative and economic conditions as will secure the establishment in Palestine of a national home for the Jewish People. To facilitate Jewish immigration under suitable conditions, and to encourage, in cooperation with the Jewish Agency, close settlement by Jews on the Land.

To safeguard the civil and religious rights of all inhabitants of Palestine irrespective of race and religion, and, whilst facilitating Jewish immigration and settlement, to ensure that the rights and position of other sections of the population are not prejudiced.

To place the country under such political, administrative and economic conditions as will secure the development of self governing institutions.

The Royal Commission and previous Commissions of Enquiry have drawn attention to the ambiguity of certain expressions in the Mandate, such as the expression 'a national home for the Jewish people', and they have found in this ambiguity and the resulting uncertainty as to the objectives of policy a fundamental cause of unrest and hostility between Arabs and Jews. His Majesty's Government are convinced that in the interests of the peace and well being of the whole people of Palestine a clear definition of policy and objectives is essential. The proposal of partition recommended by the Royal Commission would have afforded such clarity, but the establishment of self supporting independent Arab and Jewish States within Palestine has been found to be impracticable. It has therefore been necessary for His Majesty's Government to devise an alternative policy which will, consistent with their obligations to Arabs and Jews, meet the needs of the situation in Palestine. . . .

Reinterpreting Balfour

It has been urged that the expression "a national home for the Jewish people" offered a prospect that Palestine might in due course become a Jewish State or Commonwealth. His Majesty's Government do not wish to contest the view, which was expressed by the Royal Commission, that the Zionist leaders at the time of the issue of the Balfour Declaration recognised that an ultimate Jewish State was not precluded by the terms of the Declaration. But, with the Royal Commission, His Majesty's Government believe that the framers of the Mandate in which the Balfour Declaration was embodied could not have intended that Palestine should be converted into a Jewish State against the will of the Arab population of the country. . . .

His Majesty's Government therefore now declare unequivocally that it is not part of their policy that Palestine should become a Jewish State. They would indeed regard it as contrary to their obligations to the Arabs under the Mandate, as well as to the assurances which have been given to the Arab people in the past, that the Arab population of

Palestine should be made the subjects of a Jewish State against their will. . . .

Creating a Palestinian State

His Majesty's Government are charged as the Mandatory authority "to secure the development of self governing institutions" in Palestine. Apart from this specific obligation, they would regard it as contrary to the whole spirit of the Mandate system that the population of Palestine should remain forever under Mandatory tutelage. It is proper that the people of the country should as early as possible enjoy the rights of self government which are exercised by the people of neighbouring countries. His Majesty's Government are unable at present to foresee the exact constitutional forms which government in Palestine will eventually take, but their objective is self government, and they desire to see established ultimately an independent Palestine State. It should be a State in which the two peoples in Palestine, Arabs and Jews, share authority in government in such a way that the essential interests of each are shared. . . .

The objective of His Majesty's Government is the establishment within 10 years of an independent Palestine State in such treaty relations with the United Kingdom as will provide satisfactorily for the commercial and strategic requirements of both countries in the future. The proposal for the establishment of the independent State would involve consultation with the Council of the League of Nations with a view to the termination of the Mandate.

The independent State should be one in which Arabs and Jews share government in such a way as to ensure that the essential interests of each community are safeguarded.

The establishment of the independent State will be preceded by a transitional period throughout which His Majesty's Government will retain responsibility for the country. During the transitional period the people of Palestine will be given an increasing part in the government of their country. Both sections of the population will have an opportunity to participate in the machinery of government, and the process will be carried on whether or not they both avail themselves of it.

As soon as peace and order have been sufficiently restored in Palestine steps will be taken to carry out this policy of giving the people of Palestine an increasing part in the government of their country, the objective being to place Palestinians in charge of all the Departments of Government, with the assistance of British advisers and subject to the control of the High Commissioner. Arab and Jewish representatives will be invited to serve as heads of Departments approximately in proportion to their respective populations. The number of Palestinians in charge of Departments will be increased as circumstances permit until all heads of Departments are Palestinians, exercising the administrative and advisory functions which are presently performed by British officials. When that stage is reached consideration will be given to the question of converting the Executive Council into a Council of Ministers with a consequential change in the status and functions of the Palestinian heads of Departments.

His Majesty's Government make no proposals at this stage regarding the establishment of an elective legislature. Nevertheless they would regard this as an appropriate constitutional development, and, should public opinion in Palestine hereafter show itself in favour of such a development, they will be prepared, provided that local conditions permit, to establish the necessary machinery.

The independent state should be one in which Arabs and Jews share government in such a way . . . that the essential interests of each community are safeguarded.

At the end of five years from the restoration of peace and order, an appropriate body representative of the people of Palestine and of His Majesty's Government will be set up to review the working of the constitutional arrangements during the transitional period and to consider and make recommendations regarding the constitution of the independent Palestine State.

His Majesty's Government will require to be satisfied that in the treaty contemplated by sub-paragraph (6) adequate provision has been made for:

the security of, and freedom of access to the Holy Places, and protection of the interests and property of the various religious bodies.

the protection of the different communities in Palestine in accordance with the obligations of His Majesty's Government to both Arabs and Jews and for the special position in Palestine of the Jewish National Home.

such requirements to meet the strategic situation as may be regarded as necessary by His Majesty's Government in the light of the circumstances then existing. His Majesty's Government will also require to be satisfied that the interests of certain foreign countries in Palestine, for the preservation of which they are at present responsible, are adequately safeguarded.

His Majesty's Government will do everything in their power to create conditions which will enable the independent Palestine State to come into being within 10 years. If, at the end of 10 years, it appears to His Majesty's Government that, contrary to their hope, circumstances require the postponement of the establishment of the independent State, they will consult with representatives of the people of Palestine, the Council of the League of Nations and the neighbouring Arab States before deciding on such a postponement. If His Majesty's Government come to the conclusion that postponement is unavoidable, they will invite the co-operation of these parties in framing plans for the future with a view to achieving the desired objective at the earliest possible date. . . .

Limiting Jewish Immigration

Under Article 6 of the Mandate, the Administration of Palestine, "while ensuring that the rights and position of other sections of the population are not prejudiced," is required to "facilitate Jewish immigration under suitable conditions." . . .

But His Majesty's Government do not read either the Statement of Policy of 1922 or the letter of 1931 as implying that the Mandate requires them, for all time and in all circumstances, to facilitate the immigration of Jews into Palestine subject only to consideration of the country's economic absorptive capacity. Nor do they find anything in the Mandate or in subsequent Statements of Policy to support the view that the establishment of a Jewish National Home in Palestine cannot be effected unless immigration is allowed to continue indefinitely. If immigration has an adverse effect on the economic position in the country, it should clearly be restricted; and equally, if it has a seriously damaging effect on the political position in the country, that is a factor that should not be ignored. Although it is not difficult to contend that the large number of Jewish immigrants who have been admitted so far have been absorbed economically, the fear of the Arabs that this influx will continue indefinitely until the Jewish population is in a position to dominate them has produced consequences which are extremely grave for Jews and Arabs alike and for the peace and prosperity of Palestine. The lamentable disturbances of the past three years are only the latest and most sustained manifestation of this intense Arab apprehension. The methods employed by Arab terrorists against fellow Arabs and Jews alike must receive unqualified condemnation. But it cannot be denied that fear of indefinite Jewish immigration is widespread amongst the Arab population and that this fear has made possible disturbances which have given a serious setback to economic progress, depleted the Palestine exchequer, rendered life and property insecure, and produced a bitterness between the Arab and Jewish populations which is deplorable between citizens of the same country. If in these circumstances immigration is continued up to the economic absorptive capacity of the country, regardless of all other considerations, a fatal enmity between the two peoples will be perpetuated, and the situation in Palestine may become a permanent source of friction amongst all peoples in the Near and Middle East. His Majesty's Government cannot take the view that either their obligations under the Mandate, or considerations of common sense and justice, require that they should ignore these circumstances in framing immigration policy.

After [a] period of five years, no further Jewish immigration will be permitted unless the Arabs of Palestine are prepared to acquiesce in it.

In the view of the Royal Commission the association of the policy of the Balfour Declaration with the Mandate system implied the belief that Arab hostility to the former would sooner or later be overcome. It has been the hope of British Governments ever since the Balfour Declaration was issued that in time the Arab population, recognizing the advantages to be derived from Jewish settlement and development in Palestine, would become reconciled to the further growth of the Jewish National Home. This hope has not been fulfilled. The alternatives before His Majesty's Government are either (i) to seek to expand the Jewish National Home indefinitely by immigration, against the strongly expressed will of the Arab people of the country; or (ii) to permit further expansion of the Jewish National Home by immigration only if the Arabs are prepared to acquiesce in it. The former policy means rule by force. Apart from other considerations, such a policy seems to His Majesty's Government to be contrary to the whole spirit of Article 22 of the Covenant of the League of Nations, as well as to their specific obligations to the Arabs in the Palestine Mandate. Moreover, the relations between the Arabs and the Jews in Palestine must be based sooner or later on mutual tolerance and goodwill; the peace, security and progress of the Jewish National Home itself requires this. Therefore His Majesty's Government, after earnest consideration, and taking into account the extent to which the growth of the Jewish National Home has been facilitated over the last twenty years, have decided that the time has come to adopt in principle the second of the alternatives referred to above.

Many times and in many places in Palestine during recent years the Arab and Jewish inhabitants have lived in friendship together.

It has been urged that all further Jewish immigration into Palestine should be stopped forthwith. His Majesty's Government cannot accept such a proposal. It would damage the whole of the financial and economic system of Palestine and thus effect adversely the interests of Arabs and Jews alike. Moreover, in the view of His Majesty's Government, abruptly to stop further immigration would be unjust to the Jewish National Home. But, above all, His Majesty's Government are conscious of the present unhappy plight of large numbers of Jews who seek refuge from certain European countries, and they believe that Palestine can and should make a further contribution to the solution of this pressing world problem. In all these circumstances, they believe that they will be acting consistently with their Mandatory obligations to both Arabs and Jews, and in the manner best calculated to serve the interests of the whole people of Palestine, by adopting the following proposals regarding immigration:

Jewish immigration during the next five years will be at a rate which, if economic absorptive capacity permits, will bring the Jewish population up to approximately one third of the total population of the country. Taking into account the expected natural increase of the Arab and Jewish populations, and the number of illegal Jewish immigrants now in the country, this would allow of the admission, as from the beginning of April this year, of some 75,000 immigrants over the next five years. These immigrants would, subject to the criterion of economic absorptive capacity, be admitted as follows:

For each of the next five years a quota of 10,000 Jewish immigrants will be allowed on the understanding that a shortage one year may be added to the quotas for subsequent years, within the five year period, if economic absorptive capacity permits.

In addition, as a contribution towards the solution of the Jewish refugee problem, 25,000 refugees will be admitted as soon as the High Commissioner is satisfied that adequate provision for their maintenance is ensured, special consideration being given to refugee children and dependents.

The existing machinery for ascertaining economic absorptive capacity will be retained, and the High Commissioner will have the ultimate responsibility for deciding the limits of economic capacity. Before each periodic decision is taken, Jewish and Arab representatives will be consulted.

After the period of five years, no further Jewish immigration will be permitted unless the Arabs of Palestine are prepared to acquiesce in it. . . .

Controlling the Land

The Administration of Palestine is required, under Article 6 of the Mandate, "while ensuring that the rights and position of other sections of the population are not prejudiced," to encourage "close settlement by Jews on the land," and no restriction has been imposed hitherto on the transfer of land from Arabs to Jews. The Reports of several expert Commissions have indicated that, owing to the natural growth of the Arab population and the steady sale in recent years of

Arab land to Jews, there is now in certain areas no room for further transfers of Arab land, whilst in some other areas such transfers of land must be restricted if Arab cultivators are to maintain their existing standard of life and a considerable landless Arab population is not soon to be created. In these circumstances, the High Commissioner will be given general powers to prohibit and regulate transfers of land. These powers will date from the publication of this statement of policy and the High Commissioner will retain them throughout the transitional period.

The policy of the Government will be directed towards the development of the land and the improvement, where possible, of methods of cultivation. In the light of such development it will be open to the High Commissioner, should he be satisfied that the "rights and position" of the Arab population will be duly preserved, to review and modify any orders passed relating to the prohibition or restriction of the transfer of land. . . .

His Majesty's Government cannot hope to satisfy the partisans of one party or the other in such controversy as the Mandate has aroused. Their purpose is to be just as between the two people in Palestine whose destinies in that country have been affected by the great events of recent years, and who, since they live side by side, must learn to practice mutual tolerance, goodwill and cooperation. In looking to the future, His Majesty's Government are not blind to the fact that some events of the past make the task of creating these relations difficult; but they are encouraged by the knowledge that as many times and in many places in Palestine during recent years the Arab and Jewish inhabitants have lived in friendship together. Each community has much to contribute to the welfare of their common land, and each must earnestly desire peace in which to assist in increasing the well being of the whole people of the country. The responsibility which falls on them, no less than upon His Majesty's Government, to cooperate together to ensure peace is all the more solemn because their country is revered by many millions of Moslems, Jews and Christians throughout the world who pray for peace in Palestine and for the happiness of her people.

7

The United States Will Consult the Arabs and Jews on Palestine

Franklin D. Roosevelt

During World War II, the Palestine issue was of great interest to Jews around the world, and it was of particular concern to the British, who were the governing power. The situation in Palestine was of less interest, however, to the U.S. government, which was focused primarily on the war effort. President Franklin D. Roosevelt did not become involved in the issue and did not express an opinion on how to resolve the conflicting claims over Palestine. The one statement he did make is found in the following letter he wrote in response to a letter from the king of Saudi Arabia expressing concern about the Arabs in Palestine. After Roosevelt's death, partisans on both sides of the issue tried to use the letter to influence the policy of President Harry S. Truman, but the letter's content ultimately had no impact on Truman's decisions.

Great and Good Friend:
I have received the communication which Your Majesty sent me under date of March 10, 1945, in which you refer to the question of Palestine and to the continuing interest of the Arabs in current developments affecting that country.

I am gratified that Your Majesty took this occasion to bring your views on this question to my attention and I have given the most careful attention to the statements which

Franklin D. Roosevelt, "Letter to the King of Saudi Arabia," April 5, 1945, *Documents on the Middle East*, edited by Ralph H. Magnus. Washington, DC: American Enterprise Institute for Public Policy Research, July 1969.

you make in your letter. I am also mindful of the memorable conversation which we had not so long ago and in the course of which I had an opportunity to obtain so vivid an impression of Your Majesty's sentiments on this question.

Your Majesty will recall that on previous occasions I communicated to you the attitude of the American Government toward Palestine and made clear our desire that no decision be taken with respect to the basic situation in that country without full consultation with both Arabs and Jews. Your Majesty will also doubtless recall that during our recent conversation I assured you that I would take no action in my capacity as Chief of the Executive Branch of this Government which might prove hostile to the Arab people.

It gives me pleasure to renew to Your Majesty the assurances which you have previously received regarding the attitude of my Government and my own, as Chief Executive, with regard to the question of Palestine and to inform you that the policy of this Government in this subject is unchanged.

I desire also at this time to send you my best wishes for Your Majesty's continued good health and for the welfare of your people.

Your Good Friend,
Franklin D. Roosevelt

8

The Arabs Demand Independence for Palestine

Anglo-American Committee of Inquiry

As the magnitude of the horror of the Holocaust became more widely known after World War II, greater pressure was exerted by Jews in Palestine and America to open the gates of Palestine to the survivors of Hitler's extermination campaign. The Jews demanded that the survivors be allowed to immigrate to Palestine, but the British remained unmoved and adamantly opposed to opening Palestine, in part because of the vehement opposition of the Arabs. In November 1945, a committee of American and British delegates was appointed to talk to the Jews and Arabs to determine their views on the immigration of Jews and the fate of Palestine. The Anglo-American Committee of Inquiry issued its report in April 1946. The following excerpt reveals that Arabs opposed the creation of a Jewish State and demanded independence.

The Arab case is based upon the fact that Palestine is a country which the Arabs have occupied for more than a thousand years, and a denial of the Jewish historical claims to Palestine. In issuing the Balfour Declaration, the Arabs maintain, the British Government were giving away something that did not belong to Britain, and they have consistently argued that the Mandate conflicted with the Covenant of the League of Nations from which it derived its authority. The Arabs deny that the part played by the British in freeing

Anglo-American Committee of Inquiry, "Report to the United States Government and His Majesty's Government in the United Kingdom," www.yale.edu, April 20, 1946.

them from the Turks gave Great Britain a right to dispose of their country. Indeed, they assert that Turkish was preferable to British rule, if the latter involves their eventual subjection to the Jews. They consider the Mandate a violation of their right of self-determination since it is forcing upon them an immigration which they do not desire and will not tolerate— an invasion of Palestine by the Jews.

The Arabs of Palestine point out that all the surrounding Arab States have now been granted independence. They argue that they are just as advanced as are the citizens of the nearby States, and they demand independence for Palestine now. The promises which have been made to them in the name of Great Britain, and the assurances concerning Palestine given to Arab leaders by Presidents Roosevelt and Truman, have been understood by the Arabs of Palestine as a recognition of the principle that they should enjoy the same rights as those enjoyed by the neighboring countries. Christian Arabs unite with Moslems in all of these contentions. They demand that their independence should be recognized at once, and they would like Palestine, as a self-governing country, to join the Arab League. . . .

In issuing the Balfour Declaration, the Arabs maintain, the British Government were giving away something that did not belong to Britain.

The suggestion that self-government should be withheld from Palestine until the Jews have acquired a majority seems outrageous to the Arabs. They wish to be masters in their own house. The Arabs were opposed to the idea of a Jewish National Home even before the Biltmore Program [a 1942 Zionist plan calling for Jewish control of all of Palestine] and the demand for a Jewish State. Needless to say, however, their opposition has become more intense and more bitter since that program was adopted.

The Arabs maintain that they have never been anti-Semitic; indeed, they are Semites themselves. Arab spokesmen profess the greatest sympathy for the persecuted Jews of Europe, but they point out that they have not been responsible for this persecution and that it is not just that they should be compelled to atone for the sins of Western peoples by accepting into their country hundreds of thousands of victims of European anti-Semitism. Some Arabs even declare that they might be willing to do their share in providing for refugees on a quota basis if the United States, the British Commonwealth and other Western countries would do the same.

Peel's Conclusions

The Peel Commission [a commission led by Robert Peel, calling for the partition of Palestine into separate Jewish and Arab States] took the view that the enterprise of the Jews in agriculture and industry had brought large, if indirect, benefits to the Arabs in raising their standard of living. Though a very large part of the Jewish purchases of land has been made from absentee landlords, many of them living outside Palestine, it is probable that many Arab farmers who have sold part of their land to the Jews have been able to make use of the money to improve the cultivation of their remaining holdings. The improvement of health conditions in many parts of the country, while due in part to the activities of Government and in part to the efforts of the Arabs themselves, has undoubtedly been assisted by the work of the Jewish settlers. It is also argued that the Jewish population has conferred substantial indirect benefits on the Arabs through its contribution to the public revenue. On the other hand, the Arabs contend that such improvement as there may have been in their standard of living is attributable solely to their own efforts, perhaps with a measure of aid at some points from the Administration. They assert that at least equal improvements have occurred in other Arab countries, and that the action taken by the Government to assist Jewish industry and agriculture has reacted unfavorably on the Arabs. Import duties for the protection of Jewish industries, for example, are said to have confronted Arab consumers with the necessity of buying high priced local products in place of cheaper imported goods. In any event the Arabs declare that, if they must choose between freedom and material improvement, they prefer freedom.

In exasperation at the disregard of their objection to Jewish immigration, the Arabs of Palestine have repeatedly risen in revolt. . . .

So bare an outline gives only an inadequate picture of the passion with which Arabs in Palestine and in neighboring countries resent the invasion of Palestine by a people which, though originally Semitic, now represents an alien civilization. . . .

Western Influence

It is not surprising that the Arabs have bitterly resented this invasion and have resisted it by force of arms. The Arab civilization of Palestine is based on the clan; leadership resides in a small group of influential families, and it is almost impossible for the son of an Arab fellah to rise to a position of wealth and political influence. Arab agriculture in Palestine is traditional, and improvement is hampered by an antiquated system of land tenure. The Arab adheres to a strict social code far removed from the customs of the modern world, and he is shocked by innovations of dress and manners which seem completely natural to the Jewish immigrant. Thus, the sight of a Jewish woman in shorts offends the Arab concept of propriety. The freedom of relations between the sexes and the neglect of good form as he conceives it violate the entire code of life in which the Arab is brought up.

The Arabs of Palestine are overwhelmed by a vague sense of the power of Western capital represented by the Jewish population.

The Arabs of Palestine are overwhelmed by a vague sense of the power of Western capital represented by the Jewish population. The influx of Western capital and the purchase of modern equipment for agriculture and industry excite in the minds of the Arabs a sense of inferiority and the feeling that they are contending against an imponderable force which is difficult to resist. This feeling is accentuated by the fact that they realize that the Jewish case is well understood and well portrayed in Washington and London, and that they have no means comparable in effectiveness of stating their side of the controversy to the Western World. They have particularly resented the resolutions in favor of Zionist aspirations, adopted respectively by the United States Congress and by the British Labor Party. Although the Arab States have diplomatic representation and five of them are members of the United Nations, the Arabs of Palestine feel nevertheless that they have not succeeded in making their case heard. . . .

Arab Nationalism

The period since the first World War has been marked by a rising wave of nationalism in all Arab countries. Palestinian Arabs share this sentiment, and they are strongly supported in their demand for independence and self-government by all the States of the Arab League. No other subject has occupied so much of the attention of the Arab League or has done so much to unite its membership as has the question of Palestine.

Those members of the Committee who traveled in the neighboring Arab countries found that hostility to Zionism was as strong and widespread there as in Palestine itself. . . .

Moreover the Governments of the neighboring States believe that a Zionist State in Palestine would be a direct threat to them and would impede their efforts towards a closer Arab union. The chief delegate of Syria at the General Assembly of the United Nations told the Committee in London that "Palestine in alien hands would be a wedge splitting the Arab world at a most vital and sensitive point." The same witness expressed the further fear of the Arabs that a Zionist State would inevitably become expansionist and aggressive, and would tend to enter into alliance with any Power which might, in the future, pursue an anti-Arab policy. "The Middle East," he wrote, "is a vital region in which all the Great Powers are interested. A Zionist State in Palestine could only exist with the support of foreign Powers. This would not only mean a state of tension between those foreign Powers and the Arab States, but also the grave possibility of dangerous alignments and maneuvers which might end in international friction at the highest level and possibly disaster."

Chapter 2

Partition and War: The Birth of Israel

1

Palestine Should Be Partitioned into Jewish and Arab States

UN Special Committee on Palestine

The British controlled Palestine after World War I and faced opposition from both Arabs and Jews living there. Both groups were demanding independence, the Arabs on the basis of their longstanding presence there and what they believed to be wartime promises from Britain for independence, and the Jews because of the Balfour Declaration's commitment to establishing a Jewish homeland in Palestine. Violence escalated through the years as Jews and Arabs attacked each other and British officials and installations. In February 1947 the British turned the question of what to do about Palestine over to the United Nations. The British fully expected the UN to be equally stymied by the conflicting demands and made it clear that they would accept only a UN solution that would be acceptable to both Arabs and Jews, knowing that this was impossible. The British thought the UN would be unable to satisfy the parties and then allow Britain to do as it pleased. The UN appointed a committee composed of representatives of eleven member nations. The Special Committee on Palestine (UNSCOP) went to Palestine and spoke to both sides. Afterward, they produced two reports, a majority and minority recommendation. The minority (India, Iran, and Yugoslavia), leaning toward the Arab position, proposed the creation of a single federal, or bi-national, state. They acknowledged, however, that such an arrangement would be unlikely to work because it would require the Arabs and Jews to cooperate and live together in the same nation. The majority (Canada, Czechoslo-

United Nations, "UN Special Committee on Palestine, Recommendations to the General Assembly," www.palestinecenter.org, September 3, 1947.

vakia, Guatemala, the Netherlands, Peru, Sweden, and Uruguay) recognized the irreconcilability of the two sides' claims and concluded the only solution was to create two states; to partition Palestine into a Jewish and Arab state. This excerpt from the UNSCOP report explains the thinking behind the partition recommendation.

1. The Committee held a series of informal discussions during its deliberations in Geneva as a means of appraising comprehensively the numerous aspects of the Palestine problem. In these discussions the members of the Committee debated at length and in great detail the various proposals advanced for its solution.

2. In the early stages of the discussions, it became apparent that there was little support for either of the solutions which would take an extreme position, namely, a single independent State of Palestine, under either Arab or Jewish domination. It was clear, therefore, that there was no disposition in the Committee to support in full the official proposals of either the Arab States or the Jewish Agency. It was recognized by all members that an effort must be made to find a solution which would avoid meeting fully the claims of one group at the expense of committing grave injustice against the other.

> *Partition is the only means available by which political and economic responsibility can be placed squarely on both Arabs and Jews.*

3. At its forty-seventh meeting on 27 August 1947, the Committee formally rejected both of the extreme solutions. In taking this action, the Committee was fully aware that both Arabs and Jews advance strong claims to rights and interests in Palestine, the Arabs by virtue of being for centuries the indigenous and preponderant people there, and the Jews by virtue of historical association with the country and international pledges made to them respecting their rights in it. But the Committee also realized that the crux of the Palestine problem is to be found in the fact that two sizeable groups, an Arab population of over 1,200,000 and a

Jewish population of over 600,000, with intense nationalist aspirations, are diffused throughout a country that is arid, limited in area, and poor in all essential resources. It was relatively easy to conclude, therefore, that since both groups steadfastly maintain their claims, it is manifestly impossible, in the circumstances, to satisfy fully the claims of both groups, while it is indefensible to accept the full claims of one at the expense of the other.

The scheme satisfies the deepest aspiration of both [Jews and Arabs]: independence.

4. Following the rejection of the extreme solutions in its informal discussions, the Committee devoted its attention to the bi-national State and cantonal proposals. It considered both, but the members who may have been prepared to consider these proposals in principle were not impressed by the workability of either. It was apparent that the bi-national solution, although attractive in some of its aspects, would have little meaning unless provision were made for numerical or political parity between the two population groups, as provided for in the proposal of Dr. J.L. Magnes. This, however, would require the inauguration of complicated mechanical devices which are patently artificial and of dubious practicality.

5. The cantonal solution, under the existing conditions of Arab and Jewish diffusion in Palestine, might easily entail an excessive fragmentation of the governmental processes, and in its ultimate result, would be quite unworkable.

Two Plans Emerge

6. Having thus disposed of the extreme solutions and the bi-national and cantonal schemes, the members of the Committee, by and large, manifested a tendency to move toward either partition qualified by economic unity, or a federal-State plan. In due course, the Committee established two informal working groups, one on partition under a confederation arrangement and one on the federal State, for the purpose of working out the details of the two plans.

7. As a result of the work done in these working groups, a substantial measure of unanimity with regard to a number of important issues emerged, as evidenced in the forty-

seventh meeting of the Committee. On the basis of this measure of agreement, a drafting sub-committee was appointed to formulate specific texts.

8. In the course of its forty-ninth meeting on 29 August 1947, the Committee considered the report of the drafting sub-committee, and unanimously approved eleven recommendations to the General Assembly [and] a twelfth recommendation, with which the representatives of Guatemala and Uruguay were not in agreement. . . .

Plan of Partition with Economic Union Justification

1. The basic premise underlying the partition proposal is that the claims to Palestine of the Arabs and Jews, both possessing validity, are irreconcilable, and that among all of the solutions advanced, partition will provide the most realistic and practicable settlement, and is the most likely to afford a workable basis for meeting in part the claims and national aspirations of both parties.

2. It is a fact that both of these peoples have their historic roots in Palestine, and that both make vital contributions to the economic and cultural life of the country. The partition solution takes these considerations fully into account.

3. The basic conflict in Palestine is a clash of two intense nationalisms. Regardless of the historical origins of the conflict, the rights and wrongs of the promises and counterpromises, and the international intervention incident to the Mandate, there are now in Palestine some 650,000 Jews and some 1,200,000 Arabs who are dissimilar in their ways of living and, for the time being, separated by political interests which render difficult full and effective political cooperation among them, whether voluntary or induced by constitutional arrangements.

4. Only by means of partition can these conflicting national aspirations find substantial expression and qualify both peoples to take their places as independent nations in the international community and in the United Nations.

5. The partition solution provides that finality which is a most urgent need in the solution. Every other proposed solution would tend to induce the two parties to seek modification in their favour by means of persistent pressure. The grant of independence to both States, however, would

remove the basis for such efforts.

6. Partition is based on a realistic appraisal of the actual Arab-Jewish relations in Palestine. Full political co-operation would be indispensable to the effective function-ing of any single-State scheme, such as the federal-State proposal, except in those cases which frankly envisage either an Arab- or a Jewish-dominated State.

7. Partition is the only means available by which politi-cal and economic responsibility can be placed squarely on both Arabs and Jews, with the prospective result that, con-fronted with responsibility for bearing fully the conse-quences of their own actions, a new and important element of political amelioration would be introduced. In the pro-posed federal-State solution, this factor would be lacking.

8. Jewish immigration is the central issue in Palestine today and is the one factor, above all others, that rules out the necessary co-operation between the Arab and Jewish communities in a single State. The creation of a Jewish State under a partition scheme is the only hope of removing this issue from the arena of conflict.

9. It is recognized that partition has been strongly op-posed by Arabs, but it is felt that that opposition would be lessened by a solution which definitively fixes the extent of territory to be allotted to the Jews with its implicit limitation on immigration. The fact that the solution carries the sanc-tion of the United Nations involves a finality which should allay Arab fears of further expansion of the Jewish State.

10. In view of the limited area and resources of Pales-tine, it is essential that, to the extent feasible, and consistent with the creation of two independent States, the economic unity of the country should be preserved. . . .

Achieving Independence

The primary objectives sought in the foregoing scheme are, in short, political division and economic unity: to confer upon each group, Arab and Jew, in its own territory, the power to make its own laws, while preserving to both, throughout Palestine, a single integrated economy, admit-tedly essential to the well-being of each, and the same terri-torial freedom of movement to individuals as is enjoyed to-day. The former necessitates a territorial partition; the latter, the maintenance of unrestricted commercial relations between the States, together with a common administration of functions in which the interests of both are in fact inextricably bound together.

The territorial division with the investment of full political power in each State achieves, in turn, the desire of each for statehood and, at the same time, creates a self-operating control of immigration. Although free passage between the States for all residents is provided, each State retains exclusive authority over the acquisition of residence and this, with its control over land, will enable it to preserve the integrity of its social organization. . . .

The Arab State will organize the substantial majority of Arabs in Palestine into a political body containing an insignificant minority of Jews; but in the Jewish State there will be a considerable minority of Arabs. That is the demerit of the scheme. But such a minority is inevitable in any feasible plan which does not place the whole of Palestine under the present majority of the Arabs. One cannot disregard the specific purpose of the Mandate and its implications nor the existing conditions, and the safeguarding of political, civil and cultural rights provided by the scheme are as ample as can be devised.

But in the larger view, here are the sole remaining representatives of the Semitic race. They are in the land in which that race was cradled. There are no fundamental incompatibilities between them. The scheme satisfies the deepest aspiration of both: independence. There is a considerable body of opinion in both groups which seeks the course of co-operation. Despite, then, the drawback of the Arab minority, the setting is one from which, with good will and a spirit of co-operation, may arise a rebirth, in historical surroundings, of the genius of each people. The massive contribution made by them throughout the centuries in religious and ethical conceptions, in philosophy, and in the entire intellectual sphere, should excite among the leaders a mutual respect and a pride in their common origin.

The Jews bring to the land the social dynamism and scientific method of the West; the Arabs confront them with individualism and intuitive understanding of life. Here then, in this close association, through the natural emulation of each other, can be evolved a synthesis of the two civilizations, preserving, at the same time, their fundamental characteristics. In each State, the native genius will have a scope and opportunity to evolve into its highest cultural forms and to attain its greatest reaches of mind and spirit. In the case of the Jews, that is really the condition of survival. Palestine will remain one land in which Semitic ideals may pass into realization.

At the same time there is secured, through the constitutional position of Jerusalem and the Holy Places, the preservation of the scenes of events in which the sentiments of Christendom also centre. There will thus be imposed over the whole land an unobjectionable interest of the adherents of all three religions throughout the world; and so secured, this unique and historical land may at last cease to be the arena of human strife.

Whether, however, these are vain speculations must await the future. If they are never realized, it will not, it is believed, be because of defects in the machinery of government that is proposed.

2

The Jews Must Govern Themselves

David Ben-Gurion

David Ben-Gurion was the first prime minister of the state of Israel. In the following selection, he responds to the report of the United Nations Special Committee on Palestine. The committee had recommended either partitioning Palestine into two states—a Jewish and an Arab state—or creating one federal state for both Jews and Arabs. Ben-Gurion argues strongly against the one-state option, arguing that such a policy would place Arabs in control of Jewish interests. He insists that the Jews are willing and able to govern themselves and must be granted independence.

N ow final judgement is passed by the United Nations and the Mandatory. The Mandate is to end. That is the common denominator . . . dispelling the friction between the Council of the United Nations and the British Government. No one can predict how things will go in the General Assembly. It may not decide at all, but one thing is certain: the Mandate is doomed, not just the British Mandate, but the principle. There is neither prospect nor proposal that Britain be replaced as Mandatory by another Power or an international body—in either event pledged to Zionism and the principles and aims which shaped the British Mandate a quarter of a century ago.

Whether we like it or not, there is one vivid conclusion we must draw—if governance has to be in Palestine, for the sake of the immigration and settlement which are unthink-

David Ben-Gurion, statement to the Assembly of Palestine Jewry, October 2, 1947.

able in a void, it will be our very own, or not at all. That, for good or ill, is the significance of recent political developments, external, world-wide, mightier than any will or influence of ours.

The UN Recommendations

Specifically, now, as to the recommendations of the United Nations investigators.

There were eleven unanimous recommendations, of which only the first four need concern us here, for their carrying out—and the British Government has said it accepts them—entails our taking new and difficult steps, which we would not take so long as we thought that others might manage Palestine for our benefit.

The findings are these:

—Termination of the Mandate at the earliest practicable date;

—The soonest feasible grant of independence in Palestine, on the ground that the Arabs and the Jews, after a tutelage of over twenty-five years, wish to translate their national aspirations into fact, and assuredly no arrangement will be accepted by either with the slightest willingness which does not imply swift independence;

—A brief interregnum to create the prerequisites of full sovereignty;

—The transitional administration to be responsible to the United Nations, a link representing the indispensable element of compulsion where any scheme is bound to be unpopular with Jew and Arab alike.

If governance has to be in Palestine, . . . it will be our very own, or not at all.

We may dismiss the idea of a successor Mandatory. After not more than three years, Palestine is to be independent. The British Secretary of State for the Colonies announced that his Government would prepare a speedy evacuation of the army and Administration. Should there be, in the end, an unagreed adjustment, it would suggest that someone else give effect to it. In other words, British control would cease immediately a new entrepreneur came forward.

There are two proposals before the United Nations—
the majority proposal to set up two States, the minority to
set up a federal, or, in Zionist jargon, a 'bi-national' State.

A Pro-Arab Plan

The minority proposal indulges in sonorous theory concerning the assurance of equality between the two nations
and their historical link with a common Homeland, but
warrants no solid inference. Behind it, instead, is denial of
our age-long connection with Palestine. For equality between Arabs and ourselves it substitutes Arab precedence in
all things, even in immigration, and, in short, produces an
Arab State in the false feathers of bi-nationalism.

---

*Behind [the federal plan] is denial of our age-
long connection with Palestine.*

The federal State embraces a Jewish district to which
the name of 'Jewish State' is given. As to its area, to my regret I did not see the map that ought to have been annexed,
but it looks to be about that of the Jewish province under
the Morrison-Grady plan [a 1946 federalization plan proposed by Herbert Morrison and Henry Grady], though I
would not vouch for it.

There will be two Chambers: one elected proportion-
ately and therefore ruled by the Arab majority, the other
based on equal representation. To pass into law a measure
must get a majority of votes in each Chamber; if not, an ar-
bitral committee of three Arabs and two Jews would decide
and the decision become law. The President of the State
would be elected by the Arab majority of both Chambers in
joint session.

Over and above this, a Supreme Court with wide jurisdiction was invented, to interpret the Constitution, and we
know what interpretation can lead to. It would adjudicate
whether a federal or 'State' law was compatible with the
Constitution, and pronounce in cases of conflict between local and federal laws. Its judgement would be unappealable. It
would, under the Constitution, have an assured Arab majority of at least four to three. This majority could interpret and
veto Jewish 'State' laws as it pleased. The federal Government, with an Arab majority, would wield full authority in

national defence, foreign affairs, currency, federal taxes, waterways, communications transport and immigration.

We are willing, fit and ready to gather up the reins of government instantaneously.

At any moment, therefore, Jewish immigration might come under ban. Only in the three transitional years would it be guaranteed, and then into the Jewish district alone, in numbers not exceeding its economic capacity and not necessarily to the full absorptive extent; the rights of the citizens of the Jewish district would have to be considered, and the rate of natural increase. And all as determined by a committee of nine, three Jews, three Arabs, and three of the United Nations representatives.

Liability for the immigrants during the triennium would fall on the Yishuv. The Jewish Agency disappears. Thereafter, immigration is in the hands of the federal Government, as I have explained, and that is as much as to say in the hands of an Arab majority. The Arabs have lost no time in declaring that not another Jew will be let in. . . .

Jews Will Gather the Reins

The status quo cannot go on: it has been condemned on all hands. It is hard to guess when the British will actually leave—three months, three years, or thirty, there is no telling. We know of 'provisional' occupations that lasted sixty. So let us be neither over-sanguine nor cast down. We are vitally concerned that Britain should not, under any pretence whatever, keep on implementing the policy of the White Paper [the 1939 British policy statement that limited Jewish immigration]. What we want is mass immigration. The majority proposal provides for 6,250 persons monthly to enter during the transition period beginning on 1 September 1947. There is an account to settle with Britain for shutting out thousands of Jews since the White Paper appeared, and we may let history make that settlement. But a new chapter is opening—the instant chapter of what is to befall in immigration now: this month, this year, next year. For us, now, there is no countenancing the White Paper's policy one moment after the Assembly of the United Nations ends, for is it not shorn of all international sanction, constitutionally and morally indefensible?

Moreover, we must at all costs prevent chaos and anarchy ensuing.

To sum up, it is all a question of effectuation, for both the United Nations and ourselves. . . . Britain assures us she will not carry out any United Nations' decision, but neither will she resist any, so be it she is rid of the concomitant task. We, therefore, tell the world that we will ourselves discharge it, that we are willing, fit and ready to gather up the reins of government instantaneously.

We are twain—the elect of the Jewish people and the elect of the Yishuv. Alone, neither can perform the task. The Yishuv, indeed, is also a part of the people, but is so nearly concerned that it must here be a vanguard as well, as it was before in reconstructing Israel and vindicating Zionism. But this is no personal issue of us who live in Palestine. The majority on the Committee sees it as a problem of world Jewry, and so, we think, does public opinion generally.

The majority framed its conclusions under the impact of two compelling revelations. First, it found here not just one more Kehillah, but the nucleus of a Jewish nation, a Jewish State in embryo. Second, words exchanged with an unknown Jew in an unnamed camp in Europe, words that should be broadcast in every spoken tongue, a simple story of past sufferings, and of why he wants to come here and nowhere else. Thus the Committee learned that Aliyah [literally "going up"; Jewish immigration] is not shallow submission to Zionist propaganda, but a deep compulsion, elemental, mocking death. This the members saw again with their own eyes in ships that bore to Palestine the exiled and the slain, in camps that shelter those who ran the gauntlet.

This is our native land; it is not as birds of passage that we return to it.

There was, however, a *tertium quid*—and careful study of the report brings it out: the existence of an international commitment to the Jewish people, the flickering still of a spark of conscience in the world, the widespread recognition that the commitment must be honoured, even if only in part, even if only a helpless, homeless, stateless folk was its object.

All of Jewry was that object, not the Yishuv alone, all of

Jewry broke into the Land, all of Jewry seeks independence. So, too, let all of Jewry demand that an interim Jewish Government be set up to execute an interim policy under United Nations supervision and with aid thence, and primarily an interim policy of large-scale immigration and rescindment of the White Paper. If a final policy we could accept were propounded meanwhile, we should start on that likewise.

No more protests and clamour, not another day of a vacuum in theory, jurisdiction and ethics. We shall bear the grave responsibility ourselves, untried though we have been in the arts and burdens of sovereignty for the last eighteen hundred years. The strain will be terrific. There is a local pretender to the throne, backed by millions of common creed and speech. But between acquiescing in the White Paper, with its locked gates and racial discrimination, and the assumption of sovereign power, there can, in truth, only be one choice. Perhaps we are unready, immature—but events will not wait on us. The international calendar will not synchronise itself to ours. We are set the problem and must solve it. I have told you how: supervised by the United Nations, helped by the United Nations, but in our own name, answerable to ourselves, with our own resources. . . .

Relations with Arabs

This is our native land; it is not as birds of passage that we return to it. But it is situated in an area engulfed by Arabic-speaking peoples, mainly followers of Islam. Now, if ever, we must do more than make peace with them; we must achieve collaboration and alliance on equal terms. Remembering what Arab delegations from Palestine and its neighbours say in the General Assembly and in other places, talk of Arab-Jewish amity sounds fantastic, for the Arabs do not wish it, they will not sit at the same table with us, they want to treat us as they do the Jews of Baghdad, Cairo and Damascus.

That is the attitude officially proclaimed, and it is not to be scoffed at; considerable forces in the Arab realm, and beyond, are behind it. Neither should we overrate it, or be panicked by it. As Jews, and more so as Zionists, we must forego facile optimism and barren despondency. Basic facts are our allies and no concatenation of events can shake or alter them: the tragedy of the Jews, the desolation of the Land, our unbreakable bond with it, our creativity—they have brought us thus far, whether other things helped or hindered.

There are basic facts in the Arab realm also, not only transient ones, and understanding of them should blow away our pessimism. They are the historical needs of the Arabs and of their States. A people's needs are not always articulate, its spokesmen may not always be concerned for them, but they cannot be stifled for long, eventually they force their swelling way out into expression and satisfaction. . . .

A final fact. From our work in Palestine, from the society we are constructing, our economy and science, our culture and humanity, our social and fiscal order, and from no other source, must enlightenment come to our neighbours, for if they do not learn from us and labour with us, it is with strangers, potent and tyrannous, that they will find themselves partnered.

They in turn have much to give us, they are blessed with what we lack. Great territories, ample for themselves and their children's children, even if they are far more prolific than they are today. We do not covet their expanses nor will we penetrate them—for we shall fight to end Diaspora in Arab lands as fiercely as we fought to end it in Europe, we want to be assembled wholly in our own Land. But if this region is to expand to the full, there must be reciprocity, there can be mutual aid—economic, political and cultural—between Jew and Arab. That is the necessity which will prevail, and the daily fulminations of their leaders should not alarm us unduly—they do not echo the real interests of the Arab peoples.

Come what may, we will not surrender our right to free Aliyah, to rebuild our shattered Homeland, to claim statehood. If we are attacked, we will fight back. But we will do everything in our power to maintain peace, and establish a Cupertino gainful to both. It is now, here and now, from Jerusalem itself, that a call must go out to the Arab nations to join forces with Jewry and the destined Jewish State and work shoulder to shoulder for our common good, for the peace and progress of sovereign equals.

3
Declaration of the Establishment of the State of Israel

Jewish People's Council

On May 14, 1948, the day that the British Mandate for Palestine formally expired, the council of the Jews that had been the community's political authority during the mandatory period met at the Tel Aviv Museum and approved the following proclamation of independence for the state of Israel. The acknowledged leader of the council, David Ben-Gurion, became the head of state with the expectation that democratic elections would be held when the coming war was over.

EretzIsrael (the Land of Israel) was the birthplace of the Jewish people. Here their spiritual, religious and political identity was shaped. Here they first attained to statehood, created cultural values of national and universal significance and gave to the world the eternal Book of Books.

After being forcibly exiled from their land, the people kept faith with it throughout their Dispersion and never ceased to pray and hope for their return to it and for the restoration in it of their political freedom.

Impelled by this historic and traditional attachment, Jews strove in every successive generation to reestablish themselves in their ancient homeland. In recent decades they returned in their masses. Pioneers, ma'pilim (immigrants coming to EretzIsrael in defiance of restrictive legislation) and defenders, they made deserts bloom, revived the

Jewish People's Council, "The Declaration of the Establishment of the State of Israel," www.mfa.gov.il, May 14, 1948.

Hebrew language, built villages and towns, and created a thriving community controlling its own economy and culture, loving peace but knowing how to defend itself, bringing the blessings of progress to all the country's inhabitants, and aspiring towards independent nationhood.

In the year 5657 (1897), at the summons of the spiritual father of the Jewish State, Theodore Herzl, the First Zionist Congress convened and proclaimed the right of the Jewish people to national rebirth in its own country.

We . . . hereby declare the establishment of a Jewish state in EretzIsrael, to be known as the State of Israel.

This right was recognized in the Balfour Declaration of the 2nd November, 1917, and reaffirmed in the Mandate of the League of Nations which, in particular, gave international sanction to the historic connection between the Jewish people and EretzIsrael and to the right of the Jewish people to rebuild its National Home.

The catastrophe which recently befell the Jewish people—the massacre of millions of Jews in Europe—was another clear demonstration of the urgency of solving the problem of its homelessness by reestablishing in EretzIsrael the Jewish State, which would open the gates of the homeland wide to every Jew and confer upon the Jewish people the status of a fully privileged member of the community of nations.

Survivors of the Nazi holocaust in Europe, as well as Jews from other parts of the world, continued to migrate to EretzIsrael, undaunted by difficulties, restrictions and dangers, and never ceased to assert their right to a life of dignity, freedom and honest toil in their national homeland.

In the Second World War, the Jewish community of this country contributed its full share to the struggle of the freedom and peaceloving nations against the forces of Nazi wickedness and, by the blood of its soldiers and its war effort, gained the right to be reckoned among the peoples who founded the United Nations.

On the 29th November, 1947, the United Nations General Assembly passed a resolution calling for the establishment of a Jewish State in EretzIsrael; the General Assembly required the inhabitants of EretzIsrael to take such steps as were necessary on their part for the implementation of that resolution. This recognition by the United Nations of the right of the Jewish people to establish their State is irrevocable.

This right is the natural right of the Jewish people to be masters of their own fate, like all other nations, in their own sovereign State.

Accordingly we, members of the People's Council, representatives of the Jewish community of EretzIsrael and of the Zionist movement, are here assembled on the day of the termination of the British mandate over EretzIsrael and, by virtue of our natural and historic right and on the strength of the Resolution of the United Nations General Assembly, hereby declare the establishment of a Jewish state in EretzIsrael, to be known as the State of Israel.

WE DECLARE that, with effect from the moment of the termination of the Mandate being tonight, the eve of Sabbath, the 6th Iyar, 5708 (15th May, 1948), until the establishment of the elected, regular authorities of the State in accordance with the Constitution which shall be adopted by the Elected Constituent Assembly not later than the 1st October 1948, the People's Council shall act as a Provisional Council of State, and its executive organ, the People's Administration, shall be the Provisional Government of the Jewish State, to be called "Israel."

We appeal . . . to the Arab inhabitants of the State of Israel to preserve peace and participate in the upbuilding of the State.

THE STATE OF ISRAEL will be open for Jewish immigration and for the Ingathering of the Exiles; it will foster the development of the country for the benefit of all its inhabitants; it will be based on freedom, justice and peace as envisaged by the prophets of Israel; it will ensure complete equality of social and political rights to all its inhabitants irrespective of religion, race or sex; it will guarantee freedom of religion, conscience, language, education and culture; it will safeguard the Holy Places of all religions; and it will be faithful to the principles of the Charter of the United Nations.

THE STATE OF ISRAEL is prepared to cooperate with the agencies and representatives of the United Nations in implementing the resolution of the General Assembly of the 29th November, 1947, and will take steps to bring about the economic union of the whole of EretzIsrael.

WE APPEAL to the United Nations to assist the Jewish people in the buildingup of its State and to receive the State of Israel into the comity of nations.

WE APPEAL in the very midst of the onslaught launched against us now for months to the Arab inhabitants of the State of Israel to preserve peace and participate in the upbuilding of the State on the basis of full and equal citizenship and due representation in all its provisional and permanent institutions.

WE EXTEND our hand to all neighbouring states and their peoples in an offer of peace and good neighbourliness, and appeal to them to establish bonds of cooperation and mutual help with the sovereign Jewish people settled in its own land. The State of Israel is prepared to do its share in a common effort for the advancement of the entire Middle East.

WE APPEAL to the Jewish people throughout the Diaspora to rally round the Jews of EretzIsrael in the tasks of immigration and upbuilding and to stand by them in the great struggle for the realization of the ageold dream the redemption of Israel.

Placing our trust in the Almighty, we affix our signatures to this proclamation at this session of the provisional council of state, on the soil of the homeland, in the city of Telaviv, on this Sabbath eve, the 5th day of Iyar, 5708 (14th May, 1948).

David BenGurion
Rabbi Kalman Kahana
Aharon Zisling
Yitzchak Ben Zvi
Saadia Kobashi
Daniel Auster
Rachel Cohen
David Zvi Pinkas
Mordekhai Bentov
Moshe Kolodny
Eliyahu Berligne
Rabbi Yitzchak Meir Levin
Eliezer Kaplan

Fritz Bernstein
Abraham Katznelson
Rabbi Wolf Gold
Meir David Loewenstein
Felix Rosenblueth
Meir Grabovsky
David Remez
Yitzchak Gruenbaum
Zvi Luria
Berl Repetur
Dr. Abraham Granovsky
Golda Myerson
Mordekhai Shattner
Nachum Nir
Ben Zion Sternberg
Eliyahu Dobkin
Zvi Segal
Bekhor Shitreet
Meir WilnerKovner
Rabbi Yehuda Leib Hacohen Fishman
Moshe Shapira
Zerach Wahrhaftig
Moshe Shertok
Herzl Vardi

4

The Arab League's War Against Israel Is Justified

Arab League

When the British brought the question of Palestine to the United Nations, the Arabs made no secret of the fact that they opposed any solution that did not result in the creation of an Arab state in all of Palestine. When the UN voted to partition Palestine and create an Arab and a Jewish state, the Arabs made clear they would oppose the implementation of the resolution by force. Almost immediately after the UN vote, Arab attacks on Jews began. When the British decided to withdraw their forces once and for all from Palestine, the Jews announced they would declare their independence on May 14, 1948. That night the armies of Jordan, Egypt, Syria, and Lebanon invaded Palestine with the intention of destroying the newly declared state of Israel. The umbrella political organization to which all the Arab states belonged, the Arab League, issued the following statement on May 15, as their forces were advancing, outlining their reasons for using military force to prevent the establishment of a Jewish state.

---

1. Palestine was part of the former Ottoman Empire subject to its law and represented in its parliament. The overwhelming majority of the population of Palestine were Arabs. There was in it a small minority of Jews that enjoyed the same rights and bore the same responsibilities as the [other] inhabitants, and did not suffer any ill-treatment on account of its religious beliefs. The holy places were inviolable and the freedom of access to them was guaranteed.

Arab League, "Arab League Declaration on the Invasion of Palestine," www.mfa.gov.il, May 15, 1948.

2. The Arabs have always asked for their freedom and independence. On the outbreak of the First World War, and when the Allies declared that they were fighting for the liberation of peoples, the Arabs joined them and fought on their side with a view to realising their national aspirations and obtaining their independence. England pledged herself to recognise the independence of the Arab countries in Asia, including Palestine. The Arabs played a remarkable part in the achievement of final victory and the Allies have admitted this.

3. In 1917 England issued a declaration in which she expressed her sympathy with the establishment of a National Home for the Jews in Palestine. When the Arabs knew of this they protested against it, but England reassured them by affirming to them that this would not prejudice the right of their countries to freedom and independence or affect the political status of the Arabs in Palestine. Notwithstanding the legally void character of this declaration, it was interpreted by England to aim at no more than the establishment of a spiritual centre for the Jews in Palestine, and to conceal no ulterior political aims, such as the establishment of a Jewish State. The same thing was declared by the Jewish leaders.

Britain Reneges

4. When the war came to an end England did not keep her promise. Indeed, the Allies placed Palestine under the Mandate system and entrusted England with [the task of carrying it out], in accordance with a document providing for the administration of the country, in the interests of its inhabitants and its preparation for the independence which the Covenant of the League of Nations recognised that Palestine was qualified to have.

5. England administered Palestine in a manner which enabled the Jews to flood it with immigrants and helped them to settle in the country. [This was so] notwithstanding the fact that it was proved that the density of the population in Palestine had exceeded the economic capacity of the country to absorb additional immigrants. England did not pay regard to the interests or rights of the Arab inhabitants, the lawful owners of the country. Although they used to express, by various means, their concern and indignation on account of this state of affairs which was harmful to their be-

ing and their future, they [invariably] were met by indifference, imprisonment and oppression.

6. As Palestine is an Arab country, situated in the heart of the Arab countries and attached to the Arab world by various ties—spiritual, historical, and strategic—the Arab countries, and even the Eastern ones, governments as well as peoples, have concerned themselves with the problem of Palestine and have raised it to the international level; [they have also raised the problem] with England, asking for its solution in accordance with the pledges made and with democratic principles. The Round Table Conference was held in London in 1939 in order to discuss the Palestine question and to arrive at the just solution thereof. The Governments of the Arab States participated in [this conference] and asked for the preservation of the Arab character of Palestine and the proclamation of its independence. This conference ended with the issue of a White Paper in which England defined her policy towards Palestine, recognised its independence, and undertook to set up the institutions that would lead to its exercise of the characteristics of [this independence]. She [also] declared that her obligations concerning the establishment of a Jewish national home had been fulfilled, since that home had actually been established. But the policy defined in that [White] Paper was not carried out. This, therefore, led to the deterioration of the situation and the aggravation of matters contrary to the interests of the Arabs.

England administered Palestine in a manner which enabled the Jews to flood it with immigrants.

---

7. While the Second World War was still in progress, the Governments of the Arab States began to hold consultations regarding the reinforcement of their co-operation and the increasing of the means of their collaboration and their solidarity, with a view to safeguarding their present and their future and to participating in the erection of the edifice of the new world on firm foundations. Palestine had its [worthy] share of consideration and attention in these conversations. These conversations led to the establishment of the League of Arab States as an instrument for the co-operation of the

Arab States for their security, peace and well-being.

The Pact of the League of Arab States declared that Palestine has been an independent country since its separation from the Ottoman Empire, but the manifestations of this independence have been suppressed due to reasons which were out of the control of its inhabitants. The establishment of the United Nations shortly afterwards was an event about which the Arabs had the greatest hopes. Their belief in the ideals on which that organisation was based made them participate in its establishment and membership.

The events which have taken place in Palestine have unmasked the aggressive intentions . . . of the Zionists.

---

8. Since then the Arab League and its [member] Governments have not spared any effort to pursue any course, whether with the Mandatory Power or with the United Nations, in order to bring about a just solution of the Palestine problem: [a solution] based upon true democratic principles and compatible with the provisions of the Covenant of the League of Nations and the [Charter] of the United Nations, and which would [at the same time] be lasting, guarantee peace and security in the country and prepare it for progress and prosperity. But Zionist claims were always an obstacle to finding such a solution, [as the Zionists], having prepared themselves with armed forces, strongholds and fortifications to face by force anyone standing in their way, publicly declared [their intention] to establish a Jewish State.

Unjust Partition

9. When the General Assembly of the United Nations issued, on 29 November 1947, its recommendation concerning the solution of the Palestine problem, on the basis of the establishment of an Arab State and of another Jewish [State] in [Palestine] together with placing the City of Jerusalem under the trusteeship of the United Nations, the Arab States drew attention to the injustice implied in this solution [affecting] the right of the people of Palestine to immediate independence, as well as democratic principles and the provisions of the Covenant of the League of Nations and [the Charter] of the United Nations. [These States also] de-

clared the Arabs' rejection of [that solution] and that it would not be possible to carry it out by peaceful means, and that its forcible imposition would constitute a threat to peace and security in this area.

The warnings and expectations of the Arab States have, indeed, proved to be true, as disturbances were soon widespread throughout Palestine. The Arabs clashed with the Jews, and the two [parties] proceeded to fight each other and shed each other's blood. Whereupon the United Nations began to realise the danger of recommending the partition [of Palestine] and is still looking for a way out of this state of affairs.

10. Now that the British mandate over Palestine has come to an end, without there being a legitimate constitutional authority in the country, which would safeguard the maintenance of security and respect for law and which would protect the lives and properties of the inhabitants, the Governments of the Arab States declare the following:

First: That the rule of Palestine should revert to its inhabitants, in accordance with the provisions of the Covenant of the League of Nations and [the Charter] of the United Nations and that [the Palestinians] should alone have the right to determine their future.

The Governments of the Arab States have found themselves compelled to intervene in Palestine.

Second: Security and order in Palestine have become disrupted. The Zionist aggression resulted in the exodus of more than a quarter of a million of its Arab inhabitants from their homes and in their taking refuge in the neighbouring Arab countries.

The events which have taken place in Palestine have unmasked the aggressive intentions and the imperialistic designs of the Zionists, including the atrocities committed by them against the peace-loving Arab inhabitants, especially in Dayr Yasin, Tiberias and others. Nor have they respected the inviolability of consuls, as they have attacked the consulates of the Arab States in Jerusalem. After the termination of the British mandate over Palestine the British authorities are no longer responsible for security in the country, except to the degree affecting their withdrawing forces, and [only] in the areas in which these forces happen to be at the time of withdrawal as announced by [these authorities]. This state of affairs would render Palestine without any governmental machinery capable of restoring order and the rule of law to the country, and of protecting the lives and properties of the inhabitants.

Third: This state of affairs is threatening to spread to the neighbouring Arab countries, where feeling is running high because of the events in Palestine. The Governments of the Member States of the Arab League and of the United Nations are exceedingly worried and deeply concerned about this state of affairs.

The only solution of the Palestine problem is the establishment of a unitary Palestinian State.

Fourth: These Governments had hoped that the United Nations would have succeeded in finding a peaceful and just solution of the problem of Palestine, in accordance with democratic principles and the provisions of the Covenant of the League of Nations and [the Charter] of the United Nations, so that peace, security and prosperity would prevail in this part of the world.

Fifth: The Governments of the Arab States, as members of the Arab League, a regional organisation within the meaning of the provisions of Chapter VIII of the Charter of the United Nations, are responsible for maintaining peace and security in their area. These Governments view the events taking place in Palestine as a threat to peace and security in the area as a whole and [also] in each of them taken separately.

Sixth: Therefore, as security in Palestine is a sacred trust in the hands of the Arab States, and in order to put an end to this state of affairs and to prevent it from becoming aggravated or from turning into [a state of] chaos, the extent of which no one can foretell; in order to stop the spreading of disturbances and disorder in Palestine to the neighbouring Arab countries; in order to fill the gap brought about in the governmental machinery in Palestine as a result of the termination of the mandate and the non-establishment of a lawful successor authority, the Governments of the Arab States have found themselves compelled to intervene in

Palestine solely in order to help its inhabitants restore peace and security and the rule of justice and law to their country, and in order to prevent bloodshed.

Imposing Peace

Seventh: The Governments of the Arab States recognise that the independence of Palestine, which has so far been suppressed by the British Mandate, has become an accomplished fact for the lawful inhabitants of Palestine. They alone, by virtue of their absolute sovereignty, have the right to provide their country with laws and governmental institutions. They alone should exercise the attributes of their independence, through their own means and without any kind of foreign interference, immediately after peace, security, and the rule of law have been restored to the country.

At that time the intervention of the Arab states will cease, and the independent State of Palestine will cooperate with the [other member] States of the Arab League in order to bring peace, security and prosperity to this part of the world.

The Governments of the Arab States emphasise, on this occasion, what they have already declared before the London Conference and the United Nations, that the only solution of the Palestine problem is the establishment of a unitary Palestinian State, in accordance with democratic principles, whereby its inhabitants will enjoy complete equality before the law, [and whereby] minorities will be assured of all the guarantees recognised in democratic constitutional countries, and [whereby] the holy places will be preserved and the right of access thereto guaranteed.

Eighth: The Arab States most emphatically declare that [their] intervention in Palestine was due only to these considerations and objectives, and that they aim at nothing more than to put an end to the prevailing conditions in [Palestine]. For this reason, they have great confidence that their action will have the support of the United Nations; [that it will be] considered as an action aiming at the realisation of its aims and at promoting its principles, as provided for in its Charter.

Chapter 3

Looking Back at the Creation of Israel

1

The Creation of Israel Was a Miracle

Paul Johnson

In the following excerpt, Paul Johnson maintains that Israel came about partly as the unlikely result of the defining events of the twentieth century—particularly the two world wars. By eliminating the Turkish Empire, World War I transformed the notion of a Jewish home in Palestine from a theoretical idea into an actual possibility. World War II created a political climate in which the Soviet Union and the United States both considered support of Israel to be in their best interest. These circumstances—combined with the Jewish people's fierce determination not to be exterminated—allowed the state of Israel to come into existence. Johnson is the British author of *A History of the Jews*.

The state of Israel is the product of more than 4,000 years of Jewish history. "If you want to understand our country, read this!" said David Ben-Gurion on the first occasion I met him, in 1957. And he slapped the Bible. But the creation and survival of Israel are also very much a 20th-century phenomenon, one that could not have happened without the violence and cruelty, the agonies, confusions, and cross-currents of our tragic age. It could even be argued that Israel is the most characteristic single product, and its creation the quintessential event, of the twentieth century.

Certainly, you cannot study Israel without traveling the historical highroads and many of the byroads of the times, beginning with the outbreak of World War I in 1914. That

Paul Johnson, "The Miracle," *Commentary*, vol. 105, May 1998, pp. 21–28.
Copyright © 1998 by *Commentary*. Reproduced by permission of the publisher and the author.

great watershed between an age of peace and moderation and one of violence and extremism set the pattern for all that followed, and marked a turning point as well in the fortunes of Zionism. . . .

The Effects of World War I

World War I had a double effect on Zionism, transforming its program from a theoretical into a real possibility but also ensuring that the creation of the Jewish state would be bloody. Until 1914, the men who ran the British empire, though sympathetic to Zionism, were inclined to fob off Jewish leaders with schemes for developing a slice of Africa. Turkey was a traditional British ally, and keeping its ramshackle possessions together was a prime object of British policy. What put an end to all that was the fateful decision of the Turks to join the side of Germany in the war. In a dramatic speech in November 1914, the British Prime Minister, H.H. Asquith, announced: "The Turkish empire has committed suicide."

> *The creation and survival of Israel . . . could not have happened without the violence and cruelty, the agonies, confusions, and cross-currents of our tragic age.*

Immediately, a Palestinian Zion became conceivable, and what would be known as the Balfour Declaration was in train. But the British decision to end the Turkish empire in the Middle East also presupposed the existence of new Arab states as well, and inevitably brought into being Arab nationalism. It is here that [nineteenth-century Zionist thinker Theodor] Herzl's initiative and dynamism proved to be so crucial. Timing is all-important in history. No doubt a Zionist political movement would in due course have come into existence without Herzl. By launching it in the 1890's, Herzl gave the Jews, in effect, a twenty-year headstart over the Arabs. Even before the war began, Zionist leaders had been in touch with leading British policymakers, and they exploited the possibilities produced by the war with great energy and sophistication.

It is amazing, in retrospect, that the Zionists were able

to secure the Balfour Declaration—ensuring the "best endeavors" of the British government to achieve "the establishment in Palestine of a national home for the Jewish people"—in 1917, while the war was still undecided, thus preempting the postwar negotiations and settlements of national claims. By the time the Arabs got themselves organized as an international pressure group, at the Versailles Peace Conference, it was too late. They did win their Arab states, but the Jews had already gained their national home and were settling it with all deliberate speed.

But World War I also introduced unprecedented degrees of violence and extremism into the world, and these too held consequences for the future of Israel. Gone was any possibility that the Jewish national home might integrate itself peacefully with its Arab neighbors, paying for its presence in their midst by teaching them the modern arts of agriculture and commerce. The so-called Arab Revolt that began in 1936 and that was encouraged and rewarded by the British mandatory power confirmed local Arab leaders in the view that their most promising option against the Zionists was force. What had driven out the Turks and created the new Arab states could also be employed, in due course, to extirpate the Jews. This became a fixed Arab notion, so that in time, both within Palestine and across the Middle East as a whole, Arab leaders, faced with the choice of negotiation or war would invariably choose war—and invariably lose.

> *The violence bred by the searing years 1914–18 . . . decisively changed the moral climate of Europe, . . . with fateful results for the future Jewish state.*

The violence bred by the searing years 1914–18 also decisively changed the moral climate of Europe, again with fateful results for the future Jewish state. In the wake of the war, extremist regimes seized power and ruled by force and terror—first in Russia, then in Italy, and finally in Germany. The transformation of Germany from the best-educated society in Europe into a totalitarian race-state was, of course, determinative. Although the anti-Semites of Central Europe had always treated Jews with varying degrees of cruelty and injustice, up to and including murderous pogroms and expulsion, it was only with Hitler that actual extermination became a possible program. The outbreak of World War II provided the covering darkness to make it not just possible but practical.

The Holocaust destroyed by far the greater proportion of European Jews. . . . But it also united much of the rest of world Jewry behind the Zionist project.

The Holocaust destroyed by far the greater proportion of European Jews, the pool from which Zionism had drawn both recruits and moral fervor. But it also united much of the rest of world Jewry behind the Zionist project, and brought into existence the American Jewish lobby, the prototype of all the great lobbies of the later 20th century. In the perspective of the Holocaust, moreover, it became clear that Zion had to be not merely a "national home" but a refuge, and a fortress. Finally, the Holocaust spurred the Palestinian Jews (and the refugees who joined them) to create the military means to defend the citadel. If World War I created the new Zion, it was World War II that made possible the Israeli army.

In the last half-century, over 100 completely new independent states have come into existence. Israel is the only one whose creation can fairly be called a miracle.

Heroic Fighting

I observed the drama of 1948–49 from the security of an ancient Oxford college, where I was an undergraduate. Academic opinion was then, on balance, favorable to the new Zion: many dons had been brought up in the philo-Semitic tradition of *Daniel Deronda* (1876), George Eliot's novel about a young man who discovers his identity as a Jew and dedicates himself to the Zionist cause, and they welcomed Israel as an intellectual and moral artifact. But opinion was also virtually unanimous that the state would be crushed. That was assuredly the view of most governments and military staffs: the notion of the Jew as a soldier had not yet captured the Western imagination.

In 1948, the Haganah, Israel's defense force, had 21,000 men, as against a professional Arab invading army of 10,000 Egyptians, 4,500 in Jordan's Arab Legion, 7,000 Syrians, 3,000 Iraqis, and 3,000 Lebanese—plus the "Arab Liberation Army" of Palestinians. In equipment, including armor and air power, the odds were similarly heavy against Israel. Revisionist historians (including Israeli ones) now portray the War of Independence as a deliberate Zionist land grab, involving the use of terrorism to panic Arabs into quitting their farms and homes. They ignore the central fact that the Zionist leaders did not want war but rather feared it as a risk to be taken only if there was absolutely no alternative. That is why in 1947 the Zionist leadership had accepted the United Nations partition scheme, which would have given the nascent state only 5,500 square miles, chiefly in the Negev desert, and would have created an impossible entity of 538,000 Jews and 397,000 Arabs. Arab rejection of this scheme was an act of supreme folly.

In the last half-century, over 100 completely new independent states have come into existence. Israel is the only one whose creation can fairly be called a miracle.

Of course the Jews fought heroically, and performed prodigies of improvisation: they had to—it was either that or extermination. No doubt they fought savagely, too, on occasion, and committed acts that might appear to lend some coloring to the revisionist case. But as a whole that case is historically false. It was the Arab leadership, by its obduracy and its ready resort to force, that was responsible for the somewhat enlarged Israel that emerged after the 1949 armistice, and the same mind-set would create the more greatly enlarged Israel that emerged after the Six-Day War of 1967. In another of the paradoxes of history, the frontiers of the state, as they exist today, were as much the doing of the Arabs as of the Jews. If it had been left to the UN, tiny Zion probably could not have survived.

Soviet and American Help

Another paradoxical aspect of the Zionist miracle, which we certainly did not grasp at the time and which is insufficiently

understood even now, is that among the founding fathers of
Israel was Joseph Stalin. Stalin had no love for Jews; quite
the contrary, he murdered them whenever it suited his purposes. In his last phase, indeed, he was becoming increasingly paranoid; had he lived, he might well have carried out
an extermination program rivaling Hitler's. Moreover, like
Lenin before him, Stalin had always opposed Zionism. He
did so not only as a Great Russian imperialist but as a Marx-
ist, and he was consistent on the matter up to the end of
World War II and again from 1950 to his death in 1953. But
during the crucial years 1947–48, he was guided by temporary considerations of Realpolitik, and specifically by what
he saw as the threat of British imperialism.

Stalin ignorantly supposed that the way to undermine
Britain's position in the Middle East was to support the
Jews, not the Arabs, and he backed Zionism in order to
break the "British stranglehold." Not only did he extend
diplomatic recognition to Israel but, in order to intensify
the fighting and the consequent chaos, he instructed the
Czech government to sell it arms. The Czechs turned over
an entire military airfield to shuttle weaponry to Tel Aviv;
the Messerschmitt aircraft they supplied were of particular
importance. Then, in mid-August 1948, Stalin decided he
had made a huge error in judgment, and the obedient Czech
government ordered a halt to the airlift within 48 hours. But
by then the war had effectively been won.

> *Stalin ignorantly supposed that the way to
> undermine Britain's position in the Middle East
> was to support the Jews, not the Arabs.*

The fledgling Israeli state was equally fortunate when it
came to America, benefiting from a phase of benevolence
that once again might not have lasted. President Truman
was pro-Zionist, and he needed the Jewish vote in the 1948
election. It was his decision to push the partition scheme
through the UN in November 1947 and to recognize the
new Israeli state (de facto, not de jure) when it was declared
in May 1948. But the contrary pressure he had to face, both
from the State Department under George C. Marshall and
from his Defense Secretary, James V. Forrestal, was im-
mense. If the crisis had come a year later, after the cold war

started to dominate the thinking of the West to the exclusion of almost everything else, it is likely that the anti-Zionist forces would have proved too strong for Truman. As it was, American backing for Israel in 1947–48 was the last idealistic luxury the Americans permitted themselves before the realities of global confrontation descended.

Thus, in terms both of Soviet and of American policy, Israel slipped into existence through a window that briefly opened, and just as suddenly closed. Once again, timing—or, if one likes, providence—was of the essence.

2

The Creation of Israel Was a Heroic Response to Genocide

Ben Kamin

In the following selection, Ben Kamin insists that Israel came about primarily as a response to the genocidal politics of Adolf Hitler. Those who are attempting to destroy Israel threaten to undo a heroic and redemptive accomplishment. Kamin, the senior rabbi of Congregation Beth Israel in San Diego, California, recalls his early childhood in Israel at the time of its birth in order to stress his view that peaceful coexistence between Jews and Arabs is possible.

I was born in Israel just a few years after its inception in 1948. My father and mother were there, however, as the British withdrew on May 14 of that year, lowering the Union Jack over the port of Haifa, and raising the stakes considerably for the 600,000 Jews in mandatory Palestine now left to confront a host of Arab nations planning to invade and destroy the nascent Jewish state.

I remember living in that idyllic place as a child. It was long before suicide bombings, murderous plots laid out by dictators who trade oil for blood, and before dreadful skyjackings in Europe and America that somehow had something to do with the sweet osprey birds that flew about the desert of our little homeland.

Many of my classmates in the dusty village of Kfar-Saba were the children of Holocaust survivors who had been res-

Ben Kamin, "On Israel's Birthday: Today, What Does Its Life Mean?" *San Diego Union-Tribune*, May 14, 2002. Copyright © 2002 by Union-Tribune Publishing Company. Reproduced by permission of the author.

cued by Haganah soldiers like my own father, smuggled into Palestine from Cyprus and other places in the wake of the Nazi insanity. The names in my fourth grade classroom hailed from Russia, Brazil, South Africa, Germany, Poland and Yemen. We all planted onions and sunflowers in the reddish earth around the schoolyard and we sang songs in the free language of Hebrew.

The Meaning of Israel's Birth

There was a time when you could easily recite the meaning of Israel's birth, and it's worth remembering now. Israel only came into being because Europe had slaughtered the Jews and then because the United Nations had a stunning vote in its Security Council: By a tally of 33 to 13, the United Nations partitioned Palestine into two states, one Jewish and one Arab.

Israel's birth in 1948 was a heroic and healing response to the politics of murder.

The Jewish Agency, still heaving from the genocide and desperate to create a sanctuary for the exiles, agreed. The independent Arab nations, manifold times larger than Israel, declared their intention to finish what the Nazis had started. These are the facts; even as the ensuing Arab invasion of the Jewish territories served to displace the parallel victims of this blunder—the Palestinian people.

Whether or not Palestinian leaders still want that separate state or not, or even if they indeed covet the full region and would still plan to consume the sovereign state of Israel, the Palestinian people themselves still need to feel they belong somewhere—just as we Jewish children of the remnant felt we belonged somewhere back in the days following Israel's birth.

Learning from the Past

But before either one of us, Arab or Jew, can plan the future, we must learn the past. We were both always there in that land, even as the wind brought the Romans, the Crusaders, the Ottomans, the British, and so many others to help set us against each other.

My childhood memories include the thick citrus smell

of orange groves that lay between Kfar-Saba and the minarets of the neighboring Arab village of Qalqilya. We actually lived in peace; there was no fear in the air—'til the distant Egyptians and Syrians decided to exterminate the Jewish state in 1967 and suddenly every orange tree, every brook of water, every synagogue and every mosque would become a flash point.

Israel's birth in 1948 was a heroic and healing response to the politics of murder.

The death of Israel, now actively sought by hatemongers from Argentina to France to Egypt to Iran, would disavow every good instinct that was found in humankind after Auschwitz and Hiroshima.

Israel's emergence was supposed to have been accompanied with the emergence of a free Palestine in the first place; who can blame those of us in the Jewish community who truly care about the children of both Kfar-Saba and Qalqilya enough to require Israel's continuity just as much as we seek a just solution?

The parents who would send their children to blow themselves up in Jewish pizza parlors and at Passover gatherings, the men and women who would applaud the inferno of Sept. 11, 2001, and who would suggest that the Jews that made the desert green again are some kind of Nazi incarnation are people who never breathed in the fragrance of oranges across a warm valley of conciliation. They certainly never read a book that tells the true story of a people who survived and just want to live.

Chronology

1882–1903
The First Aliyah (large-scale immigration of Jews to Israel), mainly from Russia, occurs.

1896
Theodor Herzl publishes *The Jewish State.*

1897
The First Jewish Zionist Congress is convened by Herzl in Basel, Switzerland; the Zionist Organization is founded.

1904–1914
The Second Aliyah, mainly from Russia and Poland, occurs.

1909
The first kibbutz, Degania, is founded.

1914–1918
World War I occurs.

1916
The Arab revolt against Ottoman Turkish rule begins.

1917
Four hundred years of Ottoman rule is ended by the British conquest; the Balfour Declaration favors a Jewish Palestinian state.

1919–1923
The Third Aliyah, mainly from Russia, occurs.

1922
Great Britain receives Palestine as a mandate from the League of Nations.

1923
Britain divides Palestine into two districts; the eastern three-fourths of territory comprises Transjordan; the remaining territory is set aside for the Jewish National homeland.

1924–1932
The Fourth Aliyah, mainly from Poland, occurs.

1933–1939
The Fifth Aliyah, mainly from Germany, occurs.

1936–1939
Anti-Jewish riots are instigated by Arab militants.

1939
Jewish immigration is severely limited by the British white paper.

1939–1945
World War II occurs.

1945
The League of Arab States is formed in Cairo.

1947
The United Nations proposes the establishment of Arab and Jewish states in the Holy Land.

1948
May 14: The Declaration of Independence of the State of Israel is established; the British mandate ends.
May 15: Israel is invaded by five Arab states.

May 1948–July 1949
The War of Independence occurs.

1948–1952

A mass immigration to Israel from Europe and Arab countries occurs.

1949

Israel signs armistice agreements with Egypt, Jordan, Syria, and Lebanon; Jerusalem is divided under Israeli and Jordanian rule; first Knesset (parliament) is elected.

For Further Research

Yigal Allon, *The Making of Israel's Army*. New York: Universe Books, 1970.

———, *My Father's House*. New York: W.W. Norton, 1976.

George Antonius, *Arab Awakening: The Story of the Arab National Movement*. New York: Capricorn, 1965.

Moshe Aumann, *Land Ownership in Palestine 1880–1948*. Jerusalem: Academic Committee on the Middle East, 1976.

Shlomo Avineri, *The Making of Modern Zionism: Intellectual Origins of the Jewish State*. New York: BasicBooks, 1981.

Aryeh Avneri, *The Claim of Dispossession*. New Brunswick, NJ: Transaction Books, 1984.

Mitchell Bard, *The Complete Idiot's Guide to Middle East Conflict*. New York: Macmillan, 1999.

———, *Myths and Facts: A Guide to the Arab-Israeli Conflict*. Chevy Chase, MD: Arab-Israeli Cooperative Enterprise, 2001.

———, *The Water's Edge and Beyond*. New Brunswick, NJ: Transaction Publishers, 1991.

Menachem Begin, *The Revolt*. New York: E.P. Dutton, 1978.

Yitshaq Ben-Ami, *Years of Wrath, Days of Glory: Memoirs from the Irgun*. New York: Shengold, 1996.

David Ben-Gurion, *Israel: A Personal History*. New York: Funk & Wagnalls, 1971.

———, *Israel: Years of Challenge*. New York: Holt, Rinehart, and Winston, 1963.

———, *The Jews in Their Land*. New York: Doubleday, 1974.

———, *Letters to Paula*. Pittsburgh: University of Pittsburgh Press, 1972.

———, *My Talks with Arab Leaders*. New York: Third Press, 1973.

———, *Rebirth and Destiny of Israel.* New York: Philosophical Library, 1954.

Folke Bernadotte, *To Jerusalem.* London: Hodder and Stoughton, 1951.

Aharon Cohen, *Israel and the Arab World.* New York: Funk & Wagnalls, 1970.

Larry Collins and Dominique Lapierre, *O Jerusalem!* New York: Simon & Schuster, 1972.

Abba Eban, *Abba Eban.* New York: Random House, 1977.

———, *My Country: The Story of Modern Israel.* New York: Random House, 1972.

Foreign Relations of the United States 1947. Washington, DC: Government Printing Office, 1948.

Martin Gilbert, *The Arab-Israeli Conflict: Its History in Maps.* New York: Weidenfeld & Nicolson, 1993.

———, *Exile and Return: The Struggle for a Jewish Homeland.* Philadelphia: Lippincott, 1978.

———, *Israel: A History.* New York: William Morrow, 1998.

Ben Halpern, *The Idea of a Jewish State.* Cambridge, MA: Harvard University Press, 1969.

Arthur Hertzberg, *The Zionist Idea.* Philadelphia: Jewish Publication Society, 1997.

Theodor Herzl, *The Diaries of Theodor Herzl.* New York: Peter Smith, 1987.

———, *The Jewish State.* London: Central Office of the Zionist Organisation, 1934.

Chaim Herzog, *The Arab-Israeli Wars.* New York: Random House, 1984.

David Horowitz, *State in the Making.* Westport, CT: Greenwood, 1981.

Z'ev Jabotinsky, *The War and the Jew.* New York: Altalena Press, 1987.

Samuel Katz, *Battleground: Fact and Fantasy in Palestine.* New York: Bantam, 1973.

Jon Kimche, *The Second Arab Awakening.* New York: Henry Holt, 1973.

———, *There Could Have Been Peace: The Untold Story of Why We Failed with Palestine and Again with Israel*. New York: E.P. Dutton, 1973.

Dan Kurzman, *Genesis 1948: The First Arab-Israeli War*. New York: World Publishing, 1970.

Walter Laqueur. *A History of Zionism*. New York: Shocken, 1976.

———, *The Road to War*. London: Weidenfeld & Nicolson, 1968.

Walter Lacqueur and Barry Rubin, *The Israel-Arab Reader*. New York: Penguin, 2001.

Netanel Lorch, *One Long War*. New York: Herzl Press, 1976.

Richard Meinertzhagen, *Middle East Diary 1917–1956*. London: Cresset Press, 1959.

Golda Meir, *My Life*. New York: Dell, 1975.

Uri Milstein, *History of Israel's War of Independence*. 4 vols. Lanham, MD: University Press of America, 1996–1999.

Benny Morris, *Righteous Victims: The Birth of the Palestinian Refugee Problem, 1947–1949*. Cambridge, England: Cambridge University Press, 1989.

Conner Cruise O'Brien, *The Siege: The Saga of Israel and Zionism*. New York: Touchstone Books, 1986.

Daniel Pipes, *The Long Shadow: Culture and Politics in the Middle East*. New Brunswick, NJ: Transaction Publishers, 1990.

Yehoshua Porath, *The Emergence of the Palestinian-Arab National Movement, 1918–1929*. London: Frank Cass, 1996.

———, *Palestinian Arab National Movement: From Riots to Rebellion: 1929–1939*. Vol. 2. London: Frank Cass, 1977.

Yitzhak Rabin, *The Rabin Memoirs*. Berkeley and Los Angeles: University of California Press, 1996.

Howard Sachar, *A History of Israel: From the Rise of Zionism to Our Time*. New York: Alfred A. Knopf, 1998.

Nadav Safran, *Israel: The Embattled Ally*. Cambridge, MA: Harvard University Press, 1981.

Tom Segev, *1949: The First Israelis*. New York: Henry Holt, 1988.

Robert Silverberg, *If I Forget Thee O Jerusalem: American Jews and the State of Israel*. New York: William Morrow, 1970.

Christopher Sykes, *Crossroads to Israel: 1917–1948*. Cleveland: World Publishing, 1965.

Shabtai Teveth, *Ben-Gurion and the Palestinian Arabs: From Peace to War*. London: Oxford University Press, 1985.

———, *Ben-Gurion: The Burning Ground 1886–1948*. New York: Houghton Mifflin, 1987.

Chaim Weizmann, *Trial and Error*. New York: Greenwood Press, 1972.

Index

About the Editor

Mitchell Bard is the executive director of the nonprofit American-Israeli Cooperative Enterprise (AICE) and a foreign policy analyst who lectures frequently on U.S.-Middle East policy. Dr. Bard is also the webmaster for the Jewish Virtual Library (www.JewishVirtualLibrary.org), the world's most comprehensive online encyclopedia of Jewish history and culture.

Bard holds a Ph.D. in political science from UCLA and a master's degree in public policy from Berkeley. He received his B.A. in economics from the University of California, Santa Barbara. He lives in Maryland with his wife, Marcela, and sons, Ariel and Daniel.